Confluence

There are a few exceptional days in an athlete's life when their body is on song on a different level from other great days or great performances that they produce. On even fewer occasions, this happens for a sporting partnership or team. Day 1, Dusi 2014, with Siseko will be etched in my memory forever.

Piers Cruickshanks

It's hard at first to paddle with a guy you don't know. If you don't know his culture and you don't know his story or anything about him. It's hard if a guy's from a different race from yours. But that day was great. We showed the guys something out there.

Siseko Ntondini

Confluence

My Journey Beyond the River with Siseko Ntondini

Piers Cruickshanks

MACMILLAN

Thank you to ADreach for its support of this project.

First published in 2017 by Pan Macmillan South Africa
Private Bag X19
Northlands
Johannesburg
2116

www.panmacmillan.co.za

ISBN: 9781770104730
eISBN: 9781770104747

In the photograph section, unless otherwise indicated, all photographs are from the author's personal collection.

Editing by Craig Higginson
Proofreading by Sean Fraser
Design and typesetting by Fire and Lion
Cover by K4
Cover photography by Jetline Action Photo

Printed and bound by Shumani Mills Communications, Parow, Cape Town
SW64291

Contents

Dusi 2013

Tiny splashes flick up from behind the line of water in front of me. I pull on the blades, approaching the top of the weir confidently. A moment later, there's rushing water all around me and I'm scraping down the concrete slope. I brace my paddle on the right, straighten, then punch through the wave at the bottom. As I hit the aerated water, I take a tentative paddle-stroke on the right. There's nothing there. The blade's broken. In a moment, I'm under the white water, then grabbing for the boat, but it washes away from me. My legs are caught in the washing machine beneath me, kicking and floundering. The boat turns sideways, pushed by the current, and then folds in half, wrapped around a half-submerged rock. The current pulls me past it. I reach out but it's too far.

I swim for the bank and clutch into some reeds to pull myself out. Then I'm running up the bank, tripping on the uneven ground, over rocks and through the long grass. When I'm well past the boat – still trapped by the relentless current – I dive, recklessly now, in my fury and impatience, into the water. My hand grabs the tail and it swivels for a moment but then holds tight, not budging, even with my weight pulling on it. Reach by reach, I pull myself against the relentless current to the upstream side of the boat. Digging my hands between the rock and the smashed Kevlar,

1

I lift the boat. The vacuum created under the boat sucks and heaves and I'm pushed with the boat over the rock and into the current once again.

An hour later, I'm in the middle of the river. The water laps at my chest and I know I'm not going to make it. I've stopped twice to tape the boat up but the damage is too much. I won't be paddling to Durban. After pulling the boat to the bank, I start to put one foot in front of the other. One step at a time is as far as I can think. The nose catches on a branch in front of me, so I reverse, only to find it catches again behind me. I drop the boat and push it through a small gap in the thorns and brambles, clambering after it myself.

I look left and right. It's a motocross track. I turn left. I know Durban is to the left, but the entrance to the track could be either way. After twenty minutes of lugging and walking, the track does a hairpin turn and there's a tall fence in front of me. It's too far to go back, so I push the boat over the fence, nose first, and then the rest. It crashes to the ground on the far side of the fence. A dog barks. I climb the fence gingerly – through exhaustion, not care. I've walked perhaps 10 metres when the dog barks again, followed by another and then another. But they're mechanical barks, with little intent. So I push on through the bush, weary and wary of snakes. Soon the bush opens up and I'm in the middle of a junkyard, it seems. Old trucks are parked in dirt, perhaps for the last time. Then the dogs bark again. Behind me. I turn and see them rushing towards me. I hope that if I ignore them and feign a lack of interest and fear, they'll move away. Besides, I'm too tired to care much. They follow me, a short distance behind, barking incessantly. Through the bush, I reach another fence. I push the boat over it and start to climb.

The boat sinks again – although there was no other way – I had to paddle past the reeds on the left and the steep bank on the right. Once more, I pull it to the side, swimming and dragging the boat after me, but the mud is soft and deep. I push the boat and pull myself on my stomach after it. The reeds are tall, all around me. Eventually the mud feels hard enough and I'm on my knees, then my feet, dragging the boat. Then I'm walking across the neatly clipped fairways of the golf course and I know it'll be over in half an hour. I walk and walk.

Eventually, just before I reach the finish, I find the race winner, Lance Kime, standing there and waiting. He shakes my hand and I congratulate him. A worthy champion. At the finish, I float and swim across the finish line. Timekeeper John Oliver and organiser Brett Austen-Smith thank me for finishing the race. The prize-giving has been over for ages. The spectators are long gone. It will soon be getting dark. A few local fishermen look on in interest – or maybe it's just scorn.

'Well done, Piers.'

Siseko Ntondini emerges from the dusk, stretching out his hand.

'How did you do?' I ask him.

'Eleventh.'

'Bad luck. But it's good experience.'

'Sure.'

He looks at me as if waiting for something more.

'Just keep training. There are many races still ahead of you.'

But I'm not really in the mood for a chat. I want to be left alone. I want to go home.

'So, Piers …'

'Ja?'

'I was thinking … maybe, next year, do you want to paddle the Dusi with me?'

'There are much better guys.' I give a weak, half-hearted smile.

'No, but I want to paddle with you. You and me, we can be good,' he insists.

'I'd love to, but give it some thought. You're paddling so well. See if you can find someone better.'

Right now, I've had enough. My body aches and I wonder whether I'll ever race the Dusi again. I'm nearly forty. And I feel it.

PART 1

Born to Run

I sit watching Steve Andrews – middle-aged, some say 'over the hill', dark-haired and serious – as he leaves his old khaki Land Rover parked where the dirt road ends. He looks completely out of sorts here and he's obviously aware of the attention he attracts. From here, the township looks dusty and miserable in the heat of the day. He begins to follow the path and then stops to speak to a young man sitting on a rusted metal drum to the side of the path. He asks for directions. The man points towards a neat row of shacks ahead. Steve walks slowly towards them. As he gets to the top of the hill, Duma, the man he's come to see, emerges – and looks surprised to see him.

•

It's a poignant scene in the film. The actors are convincing – unbelievable, in fact. The cinematography is world-class, epic at times. Then there's the plot. The story takes us on a journey of discovery, of friendship, of tremendous growth and liberation. It's a story that can crack your heart and then put it back together again – only bigger than before. I love the story, but it's not our story. I never visited my friend in the township like that, although I would have liked to have done so. For me, our story starts a long time before.

As a kid, I was a born with a love for endurance sports. I loved all sport, but I particularly loved sports that required continuous physical exertion. Cricket was a non-starter. Hopeless at batting and a wayward bowler, I was sometimes put in a team because I was an excellent fielder – happy to run and dive to stop certain boundaries. Except under the high ball – then I was useless. Tennis and squash I could tolerate, but soccer, hockey, rugby and athletics I loved – and cross-country was heaven. At Pridwin Preparatory School, where I spent eight happy years, cross-country was not only compulsory, it was considered noble. On one weekday afternoon a week during the winter term, we were expected to run a 3-kilometre loop between some pine trees and across the grass of a local park – James and Ethel Gray Park – for house points. And we were expected to give everything. The headmaster demanded it. I felt such a sense of patriotism, loyalty and duty towards my house that, looking back now, it seems slightly ridiculous. The first time we ran at the park, it was to practise – with an older boy showing us the route. On the second occasion, we nine-to ten-year-olds were left to fight it out amongst ourselves.

I can still remember that June afternoon: two-thirds of the way through the run, I find myself in a group of three or four at the front of the pack. We reach a long downhill and I feel fresh, strong and full of running, so I stride out and pick up the pace. My little legs somehow outstretch the rest through the dip and up the other side. By the time I can see the finish line through an avenue of pines, I'm alone. I run through the shadows at the finish and our teacher, George Skews, pats me on the back.

'One!'

He counts all through the field as the boys finish. Afterwards, we're told to remember our numbers and keep trying to improve each time we run. I manage to maintain my 'one' for three weeks, but after that, for reasons I can never quite fathom, other boys seem to improve faster and finish ahead of me. But I never lose the passion for running. A significantly delayed growth spurt in high school leaves me struggling, somewhere in the middle of the school team. In my final year, I train harder than anyone else before the season and establish myself enough to make a district team and receive my school colours. Still, my passion and dedication are completely disproportionate to the results I've achieved. I keep detailed training diaries, lists of best times, scrapbooks of running heroes, and study training programmes, theories and techniques. I become obsessed.

Searching for Meaning

It's 1992. Elana Meyer recently finished second to Derartu Tulu in the 10 000 metres at the Olympic Games. Their victory lap together – arm in arm – is fresh in the minds of all South Africans. Even those who don't have a television have seen the pictures and headlines splashed across the front pages of *The Star* or *The Sowetan*.

To a passionate runner like myself, those headlines might as well have been printed on the inside of my eyelids. The mood is one of hope and exuberance in my seventeen-year-old world. At school, we're given the chance to spend the day in a work environment of our choice. I choose an advertising agency. Mom drops me at Sandton City and I find my way to the office, neatly clad in my St Stithians College school uniform. Fortunately, one of my peers, Stephen, arrives shortly after me. It's fairly disarming when the two young 'execs' to whom we've been assigned insist we lose our blazers and ties immediately – 'not in keeping with the career you've chosen', they tell us. Nervously, I consent. We spend the morning listening to anecdotes about late nights at bars and restaurants, about work days that traditionally start at nine or ten and go late into the night or early hours of the morning. Hints at alcoholic and drug-induced creativity abound. We're invited to a meeting where our enthusiastic heroes present their ideas for a Kentucky Fried Chicken advertisement to the client. The winning idea is a picture of a hand holding up a box of chicken, under which the text says, 'Up the Boks!' – an allusion to the coming rugby Tests against New Zealand. The client and the grey-haired managing director lap up the pun and our two execs grin at us. Immediately afterwards, they head for a pub lunch downstairs at the 'Bull & Grill' in the mall, and insist we join them 'for the full experience'. We make sure all signs of identification on our uniforms are hidden before self-consciously joining them for what we now suspect will be a boozy and long-winded affair. People seem to emerge from within the little pub itself to join our table and soon it seems impossible that I won't get found out in my school trousers and white shirt with my sleeves rolled up. We politely decline a beer or a glass of wine for a second and third time and tuck into a couple of burgers. I think briefly of Holden Caulfield asking the waiter to 'stick a little rum' into his Coke, but fortunately I think better of it.

The conversation swings around to the pros and cons of the advertising industry and why we should or shouldn't enter into it. A rather verbose, red-headed woman in her mid-forties expounds: 'My advice, after twenty years in it, would be … don't do it.'

'You can't say that, though …' someone immediately interrupts.

The debate rages backwards and forwards, the language indifferent to the two wide-eyed schoolboys with their cheeks full of medium-rare, ground mince. After quite some time, our mid-forties red-head gets cornered.

'So what would you do then? If you could do anything in the world, what would you do?'

'I'd be here doing this,' the more complacent of our young execs responds.

'Come on!'

'I would,' he assures us, 'otherwise what am I doing here?'

'Well, you've gotta do something,' our 'twenty-years-in-the-industry' woman answers.

'Sure – but that something could be anything. I'm here because of the choices I've made. We're all here because of the choices we've made.'

'Look,' says the other exec, 'my motto is "no regrets".'

Then, surprisingly, the red-headed woman turns to Stephen and me. 'What would you guys do? If you could do anything in the world?'

I sneak a few half-soggy potato chips into my mouth and start to chew, looking at Stephen.

'Anything?' he repeats.

'Sure. Anything in the world. What would you do?'

'You know,' Stephen starts – and I breathe a sigh of relief because it sounds like he's going to buy me some time to think – 'I was born near Kariba in Zim. My family lived there for a while and so it's a bit of a soft spot for me. I'd live on a houseboat there – fishing. It's so beautiful.'

'I've been up there once,' says the woman, 'and it is amazing.'

'And you?'

All eyes turn to me. I know that whatever I say won't sound as appealing as a life of fishing for tigerfish on Lake Kariba.

'I love running,' I start.

I'm met with bemused faces. Not a lot of fitness fanatics in this crowd, it seems – and quite a few cynics. But now that I've started I have to carry on:

'We have a lot of talented young runners in the townships, but they never reach their potential. I'd love to set up a training club – you know, with a place for the guys to live. And then I'd like to train them up – help them to be the best in the world. I think we've definitely got the talent.'

The certainty with which I say all this surprises even me.

'Really?'

'Ja – really.'

At 4pm, lunch finally winds up and we wander back to the offices. When it's almost time to go, I grab my blazer and, after a short search, I eventually retrieve my tie – which one of the young execs has donned in an ironic little joke. When I climb into Mom's Kombi and join the Sandton traffic, I have no idea of what my career path will be – but at least I know that it won't be in advertising.

Goat Races and Dodgy Knees

Less than a year later, at Wits University, I find a group of friends, similarly engrossed in and absorbed by the world of running. Steve Prefontaine, the American distance runner, becomes our icon. It's not because he ran the most unbelievable times but because his rebelliousness and never-say-die attitude capture our imagination. On 30 May, we commemorate his untimely death – although it occurred less than a year after I was born, in 1975 – when his MG Roadster overturned on a twisty mountain road an hour after he'd won his last race. Mark Ince, one of my team-mates, will refer to that date forever as 'the day the music died'. In our world, the lyrics to 'American Pie' have nothing to do with Buddy Holly and everything to do with Steve Prefontaine and the free running spirit he embodied. We also develop a series of 'goat races' in recognition of the Kenyan goatherd, Joseph Kibor, who at seventeen sold his only possession – a goat – to get to the national track and field trials in Nairobi in 1990 – taking on Olympic Champion Moses Tanui and eventually making the Kenyan team and competing at the Commonwealth Games and World Cross Country Championships.

Every Sunday afternoon, we race on the Wits track. Phillip Knibbs 'wins' the first kilometre of a major 15-kilometre road race and takes a 14-kilometre warm-down to complete the event. This becomes a bizarre tradition. We race anywhere, any time. Plans are made to race a kilometre down Jan Smuts Avenue and past the Zoo at midnight. Simon Gear and I each shave a 'W' in the back of our hair for the South African Universities Cross Country Championships. We dye our hair in the yellow and blue of Wits and run through the forests and campus of UPE, each at our limit. Hendrick Ramaala, who will go on to win, among other accolades, the New York Marathon, is there, in a league far above us and soon afterwards he starts winning major races. From our midst, the quiet, enigmatic Nic Alliwal runs an incredible 29:12 for 10 kilometres – the fastest in South Africa that year – and wins himself a scholarship to run for the Western Kentucky University in the USA.

These are glory years and I churn out the distances, training week in and week out throughout the year. I'm dubbed 'the diesel engine': not a finely tuned, high-tech machine, but consistent and relentless in my pursuit to defy my limited genetic seeding. At the SAUs track championships in Durban, I surprise myself with a personal best of 16:06 for 5 000 metres. It's a significant leap in performance and I'm ecstatic. But it's also three minutes behind Haile Gebrselassie's world record. Mark Ince finishes just behind me and 'helpfully' calculates that Haile would have lapped us twice if he'd been running that day. And sadly, at twenty years, I won't ever run 5 kilometres any faster.

For me, those 'varsity days' are some of the happiest. One early December evening, during a Johnny Clegg concert in Hall 29 on the Wits West Campus, I meet an enthusiastic girl with lovely, curly blonde hair. Shelley and I take some months before getting started, but already that night the writing's on the wall.

By 1995, I'm a 21-year-old student running through the dark on Westcliff Drive, on a cold Jo'burg winter night. The road takes me away from the street-lit safety of the Parktown and Westcliff mansions and back towards the university grounds that cut the northern suburbs safely off from Braamfontein and the high-rise slum that is Hillbrow in the mid-90s. Cars come towards me, their headlights so bright that it's difficult to maintain focus on the road in front of me. I think briefly of moths being drawn to light and being burned to death by it, but that's the least of my worries right now. My right knee hurts, and it's been hurting for a while. I side-step on to the pavement on my right, hoping that getting off the camber of the road might help. It's an old runner's trick: if you shift to running on a different camber, sometimes the corresponding shift in your body's alignment can be enough to relieve some discomfort. But this time it isn't. I run on through the cold night, carefully hopping over a dislodged paving stone, and turn up Empire Road, back towards the university. By the time I get back to the gym and change rooms on West Campus, there's a pulsating ache emanating from my right knee and I know it's an injury.

By this time, I've been running for many years. With the passion of a champion but, rather sadly, little of the talent. I'm above average – yes – but the results I've achieved have been through enthusiasm and commitment. When you run for hours every week on the tarmac, week in and week out, your body starts to take a beating. I've worked around and through minor injuries from time to time, but this injury is different. Rest does little to help: the pain just returns after each break. I see a physiotherapist who tries the 'McConnell taping technique'. McConnell's tape pulls my patella into line, which seems to help at first, but if I run hard the tape loosens. Also, I develop a skin rash under the tape. A knee surgeon tells me he thinks he has a solution, but there's also a 50% chance it will be worse afterwards. The odds don't sound great to me – and, in any case, I'm scared of the knife. I try two more physios, a biokineticist and two podiatrists. The first podiatrist sends me to buy different shoes, which make no difference at all; the second chops wedges from the Yellow Pages phone directory, tapes them together and stuffs them under the inner sole.

'Now I need you to get out there and pound for a while,' he says. 'The repetition of motion with your feet realigned should resolve the issue.'

To tell the truth, the shoe inserts do seem to help for a few runs but, soon enough, the knee pain returns. I'm 21 and I've pretty much given up on being an athlete. I'd always had the idea I'd be a half decent ultra-marathon runner in time, but the dream's dying. And then one day when I'm visiting my dentist, a new chapter starts.

The First Paddle

'**S**ay aaah.'

'Aaah.'

'Again.'

'Aaargh.'

'Okay. So how's the running going?'

My dentist, Chris Fuller, has the ability to keep a conversation going while his patient's mouth is wide open, stuffed with cotton wool and being prodded with imposing metallic instruments.

'Haven' ru' foh a whiy,' is the best I can manage.

I am so sick and tired of not being able to run. I run, therefore I am. But it seems I can no longer run. I am tired of 'running' up and down swimming pools and wearing life jackets for rehabilitation. I am tired of doing squats with a gym ball squashed between my knees.

'Why's that?' he asks.

I try to explain how around 30 appointments with six or seven different specialists across Johannesburg have led to no real improvement. I explain about the poor design of the human knee and that I've got a bone to pick with God if I ever make it to heaven. But, actually, I've still got all that offensive stuff in my mouth. I think he gets most of it – or the gist anyway because he carries on.

'Why don't you try canoeing?' And before I can protest, 'It's an endurance sport and it's easy on the knees.'

I'm really not sure. I'm a runner. But I humour him.

'How do I shtar?'

'I can lend you a paddle and a boat to try out, and you can see how you go.'

'Uh … thahs very kihn.'

'Whenever it's convenient, just pop around to my house and you can pick them up.'

A week later, on a cold but clear evening in mid-July, my good running mate Simon Gear and I offload what seems to me to be an absurd-looking craft from the roof racks of my old, red Ford Escort. The canoe is narrow and the deck is maroon. I suppose that's being polite: it's a revolting reddish-brown contraption. The whole expedition is completely out of character. I'm really not big on water sports. We carry the canoe down to the water's edge – the sun just creeping towards Northcliff Hill – and place it on the surprisingly clear water. It bobs and immediately leans precariously to one side.

'Have you ever paddled before?' A tall, big-framed guy who must be in his early to mid-thirties approaches us. We're scrawny runners. Most guys lurking around the club look tall and big-framed.

'No, never.'

'Come, I'll help you. Grab your paddle.'

I pick up the paddle Chris has leant me. I'm not sure that I need help. How hard can it be? He shows me how to place the paddle across the cockpit and I climb in and sit down on the curved white seat. The boat dodges and slides underneath me – what's that all about? I grab for the solid bank, sinking my fingernails into the mud.

'It's trickier than it looks,' he says. He's not joking either. I'm trying to work out what I'm doing wrong. Surely this can't be right. 'My name's Warren, by the way.'

I say something that sounds like 'Shyaah …' as I try to stabilise myself using muscles somewhere under my abs that I didn't know existed. The paddle knocks against the boat, which is behaving like a bucking bronco underneath me.

'Can you hold the tail?' he asks Simon, who dutifully obliges. 'So you need to hold the paddle evenly with both hands and pull through the water on either side.'

'Okay.' But I'm still clinging to the mud with my left hand. Some other guy has rocked up on the bank next to us. I suspect he's come to spectate.

'Hey. Hey, listen, you've got a *kak* coach!'

'Don't worry about him. You're doing fine.' My coach seems pretty patient to me. 'I'll push you away from the bank. Just give it a few pulls on either side. See how you go.'

I let go of the bank and wobble. Then I give a pull on the right. It's true; it's not as easy as it looks. At all. The water drips from the shaft of the paddle – a freezing drop on my lap.

'Okay, pull again!'

I pull, but the boat is determined to throw me into the water. I lean and lurch to the other side.

'Other side!'

I pull on the left. The boat seems to slide out from underneath me and, in less than a second, I'm in the water. Ice envelops me. Then I'm an ungainly orca, shooting through the surface, gasping for air. I grab boats and paddles and whatever else is in reach and rush for the bank in the biting, waist-deep water.

'No one's laughing here on the bank because we've all been there,' says Warren helpfully.

I nod. Simon looks as if he's trying not to laugh.

'Like I said, it's more difficult than it looks.'

'Sure is,' I agree. But I'm thinking something more like, 'This is bull dust; who can even do this?'

'You've just got to keep trying. You'll eventually get it. Like riding a bicycle.'

I wonder if riding a bicycle was this difficult when I was five. I doubt it. I spend the next twenty minutes making a few attempts at paddling the stubborn horse, but soon I'm shivering and too cold to paddle – and more than a little bewildered at the challenge. Simon and I empty the boat a last time and throw it on to the Escort's racks.

'Shit,' I say.

'Ja.'

'My fingers are blue.' I hold them up. 'And yellow.'

Simon has a look. 'Shit,' he agrees, raising his eyebrows.

Driving home, I realise this is going to be one hell of a task.

But three days later I come back. The highveld wind is blowing right through me but I manage to paddle the length of the dam – nearly 500 metres – only falling out three times. On the way back, I fall out once. Once my T-shirt's wet, it sticks to me, holding the cold tight against my chest. Soon I figure out that losing the T-shirt altogether is actually less cold. A fisherman on the bank looks at me in horror – an asylum escapee? Two weeks later, I make it around the dam without falling in. By spring, I can paddle. When I do occasionally fall in, it's not so cold. And some time in early October someone tells me that the boat I've been using is far too unstable for a first boat.

The First Dusi

'**W**hoah!'

The water jumps and swirls as I lift the boat and pour the offensive water out of it. The whooping is some other paddler scrambling for his boat and paddle. He's washed up against the same flat rock on which I'm standing.

'You almost made it! You were through the difficult part!' shouts a guy in the front of a K2, floating cheerfully past. I know him. It's Peter Wise, the friendly gent who repaired my boat after I'd mauled it down my first river.

I'm annoyed at my incompetence, but the other guy who's landed up on my rock seems oblivious to this – and is glowing with excitement.

'Hey!' he shouts, to no one in particular. 'That was a cool one!'

'It caught me out too,' I tell him.

'It's been great, though, hey?'

I can't remember having met such enthusiasm before. Especially when he must be nearly as tired as I am.

'And we're nearly there. Can't be far to go now.'

I'm climbing back into my boat.

'You also doing your first one?' he asks.

'Ja, it's been amazing.' And it really has.

'It's an incredible race this. Incredible!'

We're back on the fast-flowing water now, the river swirling and shifting our boats through the channels and hyacinth islands.

'I shot everything,' he shouts, 'and you?'

'Ran over Burma Road. It was hectic. Wet and slippery. Had to pull myself up the one stretch using the barbed-wire fence!'

And so I meet Brad Fisher. Right there on the final day of my first Dusi. It's seven months since I first fell out of a canoe and I'm still falling out, but at least now there's an excuse – the water's rushing through rapids, over rocks and around islands. And I'm here, taking part in the biggest race in the country, completely submerged into a new sport and new challenges – sharing the adventure with a stranger. Neither of us has any idea of the friendship that we'll enjoy in the two decades ahead. We have no idea that five and a half years later we'll line up at Nagle Dam – just 20 kilometres northwest and upstream on the same river system as this – and that we'll startle the established paddling community with a performance that will take us to the World Cup in Denmark and earn Brad his coveted chance to pull a green-and-gold vest over his head. Nor do we know that many years after that we'll meet with some of the leading figures of the South African film industry and that they'll leap at the story we've got to tell. But – for now – I pack myself back into my boat, pull my splash cover over the cockpit and paddle for Durban ...

The first time you do the Dusi, the guys tell you you'll see the buildings on Durban beachfront and then you know you're close to home. So I paddle down the river, scanning the hilltops ahead for buildings – and reflecting on the three-day adventure. I'd started the race underprepared and completely inexperienced.

'So how're you going to get the experience if you don't do it?' the mechanic who'd just serviced my old Ford Escort had asked. Fair point. That was when I decided I'd do the race. Well, I'd try anyway. I'd realised through chatting to the more experienced crowd at the club that it wasn't so much the physical endurance that would be my biggest challenge in the race – it was the danger of falling out in the rapids and breaking or losing my equipment. My goal was to try to finish at least the first day, enjoy the experience and see what it was all about.

My girlfriend Shelley, my good mate Anton Fatti and I pile into my Ford Escort and take the journey to Pietermaritzburg with plenty of energy but little knowledge of what to expect. Air conditioning in cars is still reserved for more luxurious models in those years and we start to cook shortly after Harrismith. We turn the fan up and spray water in our faces, but it turns out to be good conditioning as the Dusi that year would be the hottest ever raced.

I start at 10am in 'J' batch – well ensconced with the 'Fish and Chips', as the less competitive paddlers are known. An hour into the first day, I am running with my boat crashing against my shoulder, past the sugar-cane fields at the rural outskirts of Pietermaritzburg, and I can't quite imagine enduring three days of this madness. The sun is cooking! But later I reach a water point at a place called Geoff's Road and another paddler tells me that we're past the halfway mark for the day and my spirits lift. It's tough, but I'm managing. There's a camaraderie among the field of paddlers that I find reassuring. When I get to the end of the first day, I remain sitting in the canoe, astonished at the experience I've just enjoyed – the rapids, the steep hills and the heat. It is also so hot that the thought of bundling unshowered – since there are no showers – into a sun-baked tent with Shelley and Anton is preposterous. That evening, it pours with rain. The camp site becomes a slosh of mud, littered with the flotsam of ground fibreglass powder and hardened globules of resin. But at least it's cooler. We take refuge in the tent, which is dry, warm and fairly clean. I sleep like a baby. In the morning, I am delighted to be paddling away from the grubby camp and leaving Shelley and Anton to negotiate the muddied, over-crowded dirt roads in the Ford Escort.

The young human body is an incredible facility. For three days, my body will endure – enjoy, even – the assault of the portages, the rapids and the general exposure to the elements. The second day is wonderful. It's overcast and when I reach the confluence with the Umgeni River, the cleaner water forms a distinct line as it joins the muddied Umsindusi. I've studied a map but it all looks different out there and I shoot rapid after rapid. Amazingly, I stay in my boat. Every time I see someone get out of their boat, I follow them in fear that it's one of the big rapids

– Washing Machine, Tombi, Hippo. I've heard and read all the names, but I'm basically clueless – paddling on passion and with a great deal of ignorance. But the river gods are smiling on me and I stay in my boat.

The valley becomes more and more remote and eventually I see a line of boats being carried up what can only be the feared Ngumeni Hill. Now I know where I am again. The dirt path twists its way between acacia trees and past little mud huts and kraals. At the top of the path, the hills spread out in layers on both sides of the valley and the view is magnificent. Enormous rock domes burst through the thick bush, forming steep hills and valleys, dotted with little huts, as far as the eye can see. Back down at the bottom of the hill, the river is immediately threatening, pushy, angry. I pull to the side, ramp a rocky slab and clamber over giant soccer-ball boulders. Higher up the hill, I find a contour path from which I can count the big rapids – knowing that I must pass Gumtree, Tombi and Hippo before going anywhere near the river again. All the rapids down there look big to me, though.

Eventually, my legs start to get tired and I see flat pools of water below – so I head back towards the river. I find a confident-looking pair of veterans with a green Dusi Rat sticker – signifying at least ten medals on their boat – and tuck in behind them. When they stop to rest, I stop to rest. This is how I make my way through by far the biggest stretch of rapids I've ever paddled. Eventually, I get to the headwaters of Inanda Dam and I know I'll make it to the end of the second day. I will write in my diary that night that I passed 27 boats in the 9 kilometres across the dam.

That night, the camp site is prettier than the first – more spread out. But muddier too, with the incessant drizzle. Shelley and Anton have stories to tell of the search for the overnight stop and the Ford Escort almost backsliding into a ditch when the road was too steep. My stomach feels sore but I can't tell if it's from processing fluids or from my core being worked over by the river. I've drunk about 7 litres and I've yet to take a leak. Even with the cloud cover, this valley's hot. And humid. I make a mental note that a strong core is essential in this race. And so are proper nutrition and hydration. Everything in the camp is damp or sludge. Or both. But I'm ecstatic to be a part of it all.

In the morning, I'm tired but I wander down to the dam to watch the leaders set off for Day 3. Mark Perrow has made up two minutes and opened another five on John Edmonds – the Day 1 overnight leader. He stands, paddle in hand, on a small peninsula, framed by two parked helicopters, reading an unfolded letter, waiting for his start. He looks like a gladiator – set for combat. But when he sees me, he wanders over and asks me how it's going.

'Great,' I tell him, 'I'm loving it. It's a crazy adventure.'

He smiles and nods. His mind's really on the race, but he manages to say, 'Good. I'll need help to carry on giving these Natal boys a hiding next year!'

I chuckle quietly when I see he's said it just loud enough for John Edmonds to hear. Some time later, after slightly more than half the field has left, I lead my batch across the dam. But before I even get to the portage, my pedal system comes loose and I lose valuable time finding a stray nut and refixing it. I'll have to stop in the final rapid of the day to fix it again – but nothing can taint my elation. I somehow believe by now that I'm going to finish the race.

On the third day, beneath the dam wall, the water is clear and Sprite-white spray rushes past me. The nose swings quickly downstream and I can't quite believe my luck. The river is noticeably cleaner and the rapids seem almost continuous. What a privilege to paddle here. I've learned the names on the map again – Tops Needle, Side Chute, Umzinyathi. When I'm sure I definitely must've passed Umzinyathi rapid for certain (for the third time – there are so many rapids), I see a paddler getting out ahead for what must be the much-hated Burma Road portage. In the slippery, drizzle-induced mud, it is truly nearly impossible to lug my boat up the pathway. I throw it over the barbed-wire fence and try walking on the long grass, pulling myself with one arm up the wire strand. My wet, shrivelled granny-skin slips unhelpfully on the thin grey line. Eventually, I'm back in the river, relieved but exhausted. At a small, nondescript rapid, shortly after that, I fall out. Another novice, Brad Fisher, does the same.

When I cross the finish line, the sense of accomplishment emerges from Blue Lagoon in an enormous wave of euphoria. I am so happy to have made it. Not many results in my paddling career in the twenty years to come will compete with the pure joy of that day. I lie back on the beach that night and stare at the heavens. Shelley – my wife-to-be – at my side, my stomach full of pizza and beer. Finally, I don't care if I never take part in another road-running race.

A Pristine Valley

The first year of canoeing is an extraordinary adventure. Every race is on a new river, in a new, sometimes remote valley. It's true that the Dusi is the most famous race, but there are so many others to enjoy. The 'Umko' on the Umkomaas River embodies the sport perhaps the best. In my first season, I've shown enough promise and quiet determination to be assigned to 'the maestro' of the Umko: Stan Freiman. As a past winner of the race, I'm informed he'll guide me safely through the treacherous and terrifying rapids to a certain top-ten finish.

I take a look at Stan before we climb in for our first session together and I'm astonished at his apparent lack of physical fitness. They call him the 'Water Buffalo' and I can see why. But when we actually start to paddle, I'm amazed by his power and dominance of the boat – and later the river.

We descend into the Umko valley down the dirt road to Hella Hella. The giant tree ferns stand tall in the kloofs on either side of the dirt road. The 4x4, which has been full of pre-race banter and good-natured tomfoolery, is suddenly disarmingly quiet. And it makes me nervous. Before the start, my naiveté is exposed as we discover that I've neglected to drill a hole in the deck of the boat through which to access my juice pipe. Stan seems unfazed and sends our driver – Simon Gear, who has selflessly given up his weekend to watch this sport unfold – 'to find something with which to make a hole'. A few minutes later, he returns with a large, blunt panga, a small plastic fork and, fortunately, a hand drill. As we line up for the race, we're informed that the rescue helicopter thermometer reads 50 degrees centigrade. As if we didn't know it was hot. The gun fires and we're off down the river, immediately into a bustling set of rapids that Stan negotiates with aplomb. The major rapids are numbered one to eight, but many a novice has shouted 'what number are we on?' in the approaches to number one. The rapids are that big. We pop up from number one, equipment and egos intact, and pass the floating boats, paddles and helmets of innumerable casualties.

'Great driving,' I shout. But the Water Buffalo is concentrating, head down, breathing in the hot air in heavy gulps.

We're hopeless on the flat water, being passed by lighter, fitter crews, but we make up time through the rough water of the rapids. The hills and cliffs of the Umkomaas valley are remote, untouched and impressive. The steep mountains seem to tower hundreds of metres above us at some points. And the acacia forests make for some pretty spectacular African images. By the time we reach the bottom of number eight rapid – all the big ones behind us – I'm having a blast. I'm loving every moment – the scenery, the rapids and the racing – although admittedly I'm a little frustrated by the latter. We have over an hour to go as we reach the long, flat pools towards the end of the first day and I soon realise that the Water Buffalo is a spent force. At a small, somewhat innocuous little rapid, he tips us out and floats to the eddy at the bottom.

'Sorry,' he explains, 'I just had to cool off.'

I'm incredulous – it *is* a race – but I try to feign indifference. I gather the paddles, throw them on the bank and empty the boat while the Water Buffalo wallows in the shallows.

That night, we are required by the rules to stay in the valley. The organisers have set up a marquee and when we get off the water we lay down mattresses and sleeping bags, which have been transported there by truck. I've been warned that the Water Buffalo snores impressively so I quickly place my foam mattress in a gap next to six-time champion Robbie Herreveld. I learn that canoeing is not a sport of airs and graces as he chats happily but modestly about the techniques of paddling in big water. Later, I lie in a stream, trying to cool off from the heat and humidity of the valley, and wonder if I will ever get to the top of the sport. I can paddle fast and for long, but when it comes to a race where experience counts, I'm mediocre – lucky to be shuffled into a boat with the Water Buffalo while Robbie Herreveld wins the race with veteran Graham Monteith – whom I can already challenge on the flat water.

Submerged into the Ethos

The camera pans out and the boat becomes smaller on screen. Seen paddling across the magnificent Inanda Dam from above, it's Steve and Duma, chasing tenth place in the Dusi. They're into the top twenty, having been back in sixtieth after starting in the third row and losing a paddle. They paddle in perfect unison and, from above, you have no idea that it's Andile and I as body doubles on a film set. But the effect is perfect. It's soul-paddling. A boat on the water, and nothing else matters.

•

I soon find that the paddling community is pretty intimate. Probably around 5 000 paddlers in the country register and paddle in river races every year. There's also surf-ski paddling on sit-on-top boats, similar to the single and double seater canoes used on rivers (K1s and K2s) but designed for the sea. It's a sport truly in the elements and in touch with nature. There are probably as many who paddle 'now and then' or even fairly regularly but don't really race. There are plenty of those who have dabbled in the sport or who ride mountain bikes now. Then there's canoe polo – a crazy crowd playing water polo in tiny, manoeuvrable little boats. And then there are the white-water kayakers – a distant look in their eyes as they think wistfully of the last waterfall or the next crazy descent they're planning. But there are only a few who are complete ex-paddlers. They still carry something of the spirit of the sport with them. As Warren told me on that first day – it's like riding a bicycle. You'll never completely forget.

The little 'pond' that is Emmarentia Dam in the centre of Johannesburg's northern suburbs is home to Dabulamanzi Canoe Club. In the mid-1990s when I start paddling, it is the site of a great rivalry between Wits Canoe Club and Dabulamanzi. A rivalry that has already resulted in a great number of versatile athletes by then and even eventual Olympic sprinters like Mark 'Hophead' Perrow and Alan van Coller. It has also produced a whole crop of South Africa's top flat-water and river-marathon paddlers – Robbie Herreveld, Graham Monteith, Neil Evans, Michael 'Cheesy' Cheeseman and Graham 'Tweet' Bird. We had no idea of this at the time, but on that nippy Tuesday afternoon, when Simon and I stumbled down to the water's edge, we were placing that old fibreglass boat onto the most competitive body of water in the country. That community would soon come to absorb me and my dreams.

Over the next few years, the Wits Club adopts me. It turns out I am one of the only up-and-coming youngsters keen to put my head down and train just to be better. I don't need a goal or a race, I just want to be good. I've already been an athlete for nearly ten years and I know that I have a good set of lungs and a big, strong heart. I wasn't built to be a K1 sprinter, but I have a fair helping of natural endurance and I soon find I have pretty good rhythm in the boat. It's something Shelley has always been surprised by – given my ineptness on the dance floor. But rhythm in the boat – the 'feel' for the boat that paddlers talk about – is something you can't quite describe in words or put your finger on exactly. Some paddlers just have it more than others.

I will later wonder how much talent lies undiscovered because people just don't have the opportunity or inclination to try things that they might be naturally good at. I might never have been a top runner, but already I can see the top of the sport that is canoeing – in South Africa – and I have a sense that people in the paddling community think I could be really good at it.

Soon I discover that an important pillar of the training culture on the highveld at that time is the weekend Vaal session. Early on Saturday and Sunday mornings, we bundle four or five at a time into cars and head out to a quiet, flat section of the Vaal River to train. The banks are lined with tall, exotic trees with leaves that turn a beautiful yellow and orange in autumn. It feels like a thin line of European beauty cutting through the industrial edge of places called Vereeniging and Vanderbijlpark. And, come to think of it now, Sharpeville too. We paddle two to four and occasionally even five hours on the meandering river. It might or might not be the best training but it's an entrenched part of the culture at the time, with its roots in the challenge of the Berg River Marathon – a 240-kilometre, four-day race in the Cape. If you want to make it in the sport, you have to be there, throughout winter, to walk your boat across the frost-covered grass before the sun rises on a Sunday morning.

I also find that these sessions work for me. On one of these mornings, it's precisely zero degrees on Monty Monteith's Audi's thermometer – which, he assures us, is the most accurate in the country – when we arrive. Alan van Coller stops on his way to the water's edge to urinate, nonchalantly, on his feet – to warm them up. Only once pushed does he give his matter-of-fact explanation: he reckons it's a win-win solution. He gets to take a leak *outside* of his boat *and* warm his feet up at the same time. Alan will go on to two Olympic Games, once making the final – sprints are an Olympic discipline, the marathon is not. But I know him as the most unassuming national champion and Olympian I have ever met. He's an inspiration and I'm like an excited puppy, just happy to rub shoulders with guys like him.

The mist steams off the water when we push off from the bank. The trees have lost interest in their pretty autumn display and have succumbed completely to the barren grey of the winter highveld. We separate into two groups of four, two tight diamonds. A bunch of four boats is the most efficient group. One paddler in front pulls hard while the ones on each side of him 'ride his slip'. A bow wave comes off the front boat and the boats slightly back and to the side of him can 'surf' this wave. The fourth boat tucks in directly behind the front one – in the diamond – effectively riding both of the bow waves of the boats on either side of that front boat. If he gets it just right, he needs to paddle at around 60% of the effort of the front boat for the same speed – because of the wave riding. So, in our little groups of four, we head upstream first – adhering to one of the many unwritten laws of paddling etiquette that are never explained. They're just intrinsically assumed.

Upstream first. The mist lingers, forming a thicker blanket across the river up ahead. Scrawny arm-branches of trees on the banks grab at the wispy-white streaks. Monty pulls first. He always does. Not only that, as I've quickly learned, he 'tears the arse right out of it' – a wonderful description well used in a community that finds no need for reserve in its jargon. He starts at a pace I know that I, for one, certainly can't paddle at for an hour, let alone the planned three hours. I scratch around for the side wave, catching a few icy splashes on the deck at the same time. We rotate the configuration every kilometre, taking turns 'pulling' at the front of the group. Soon I find my rhythm.

A while later, the river takes a turn to the north and we enter a pocket of thicker white mist. Eventually, it's so thick we can see only our group of four boats and our own reflections off a few metres of glassy water surrounding us. The rest is an off-white cocoon in which we seem to be floating – the only four people in the world. I look around at three of the most accomplished paddlers in the country whom I've got for company – Monty, Cheesy, Hophead and ... me – the complete rookie. Even that title's a little presumptuous at this stage. There are little husks of ice on my splash deck now but I'm just happy to be a part of it all. I'm learning from the best.

Green and Gold

The seasons become a predictable loop. The races keep coming around and every year my results improve. On 27 May 1999, a Sunday morning, I wake up with that 'kid's birthday' feeling. It's a special day for me, but it's not my birthday. I've made the South African team to go and paddle at the World Marathon Championships in Hungary, and I'll wake up every day for the next few weeks with that same feeling.

Six weeks later, I'm in Györ, a city on the Danube – twenty minutes from Budapest. It's hot and humid. The water of the Danube is the colour of weak tea. It's warm and appealing, though. When I first get to the course, Len Jenkins, our Junior Team hopeful, is practising portages – and soaking up the sun and the challenge. He can jump out of his boat, run with it and re-enter at a pace I have never seen before. He is, in fact, giving us all a premonition of how he's set to revolutionise the sport in our own country. In his race, two days later, against three Hungarians, he manages to overcome a tactical manoeuvre that sees him forced to fourth at the start of the last portage, producing an inspiring effort to claim the silver medal. The other junior in the team is a young coloured guy by the name of Ryno Armdorf, who paddles his heart out, no less impressively, further back in the field. He's travelled a journey since his days of borrowing boats on a little dam outside Stellenbosch and knows nothing of the significant role he will play in the sport in the decade to come. Hank McGregor, at only twenty years old, is the number one K1 paddler in our senior team. He's tall and imposing. He and his dad strut around the course in Levi's jeans and bare torsos – an impressive illustration of genetic theory if ever one was needed. At 25, I'm older but far less experienced. Even Len, the junior, has been paddling for slightly longer than I have.

I have already got myself into trouble for choosing a team boat to paddle before Hank arrived at the course. Team manager Brian Longley reckoned I could go ahead and choose one. I had stared at the two carbon boats for a few minutes, eventually choosing one on gut feel. Hank's extroverted and involved dad – an undeniably brilliant and successful athlete himself, and a character I will always find enigmatic yet imposing – reprimands me for the error of my ways. And he has a point – I could have waited. I make my own point of approaching Hank and offering to swap boats. He laughs good-naturedly and waves off my apology. We soon discover that both of the boats have a porous section in the nose – a manufacture flaw. They've got pumps to extricate the water so we might be all right, but Hank's looks worse than mine. His father finds a hardware store and, through a little interpretation and more than a little guesswork, buys some lacquer spray in an attempt to fix the problem.

When I pull the green-and-gold vest over my head, I believe with every ounce of my being that nobody can out-paddle me on that day. I have no idea how wrong I am, but I have a sense of pride and patriotism, of immense privilege and fierce determination. A few minutes before 1pm, we line up. The tails of our boats sit neatly against the fold-out jetty and each of us locks a carbon paddle blade into the water. We are 40 boats – one of the largest fields assembled at a World Marathon Championship to date. The nervous tension is palpable. For a moment, the world is quiet. There's only me and a calm corridor of water receding from the pointed nose of my boat. Then the world explodes. Twenty seconds after the race starts, I'm in shock. Boats seem to be shooting past me, forming an impenetrable triangle in front. I'm left negotiating the choppy leftovers, scratching around at the back of the pack. But I'm determined to make up ground, believing my endurance will pull me through when the others begin to tire, and I paddle at my limit for nearly fifteen minutes, my forearms tightening in the choppy wasteland. When we turn the first buoy, I see that Hank has found his way up to the front pack – most impressive. By the time I get to the turn, I'm virtually spent – and making no impact on the paddlers in front of me. The next two and a half hours of racing are a blur as I struggle to keep out of the current heading upstream and then to find the fastest-moving water downstream. I'm frustrated by the other paddlers, who seem intent on racing against me rather than working together to make up time on the field ahead.

I end 31st out of 37 finishers – a few seconds behind the great Thor Nielsen, but ten minutes off the winner, Ivan Lawler, and the real race. I'm tired, frustrated and, quite frankly, astounded at the standard of international paddling. I had assumed that the South African team would be more competitive – the juniors are, the seniors aren't – and I realise that I still have much to learn about the sport.

PART 2

A Spark is Ignited

During the summer of the year I start to paddle, I am totally unaware that another spark is being ignited – around 1 300 kilometres away, on an even smaller body of water, on the outskirts of Stellenbosch. Scraps of the story will filter through to me much later and it will be many years before I can piece it together in a way that might be close to the real events. By the time I meet the main protagonists, they are already competitive paddlers – each with their own pedigree in the sport.

Angus McIntosh is angry. He isn't the sort of young man who enjoys being made fun of, and that is exactly what has been happening. Since the beginning of that summer, he and the other members of the Stellenbosch University Canoe Club have been arriving at the dam to find their boats still wet, in the wrong racks and sometimes just left lying on the ground. Things had come to a head in November, when they arrived at the club only to find their boats already out on the water – a bunch of coloured kids from the local farm playing in them at the far side of the dam. The students ran after the 'little buggers', but they gave themselves away too early. The kids swam to the bank and made a dash for the fence. Angus was first under the fence and not too far behind – the sheer length of his stride enough to whittle down their lead. But the vineyards of Vredenheim come all the way to the fence in that corner of the farm and the kids were smart. They scampered, perpendicular to the vineyard lines, barely breaking stride, so that within moments the students were left, ducking and scrambling in the weeds and dust – a distant shout in the background. Amongst the kids, the fear of the chase turned quickly to relief and then gleeful laughter.

Things came to a head one Friday morning when four Stellenbosch 'Maties' decided to skip their lectures and get to the dam early. They sat quietly inside the old clubhouse, threatening deeds of bravado. Despite being the natural leader of the group, Angus kept fairly quiet – brooding, keeping his thoughts to himself. Soon he would stand face to face with the culprit – a young, eleven-year-old coloured boy from the neighbouring farm called Ryno Armdorf.

Ryno should have looked scared, but he didn't really. It wasn't only that Angus was angry, he was also six feet tall and muscular. His tightly cropped hair accentuated his robust, angular features. Angus came from a well-established farming family – from a time, as the cliché says, 'when meat was cheap' – and it showed.

'I was wondering if you minded us please borrowing your boats today?' said Ryno.

'What you mean is, you were wondering if we minded you using our boats and then leaving them lying around,' said Angus.

'No, just for today.'

'We know it was you.'

'What was?'

'It was you guys who've been taking our boats without permission these past months. No one else comes here.'

'No, *baas*.'

'I'm not your *baas*. And enough of that. Listen, I've got an old boat you can use. But the deal is that you put it away when you're finished. We can't have you guys coming here and leaving this place a mess.'

'Sorry, *baas*. Thank you. We appreciate it. Really.'

'Come, I'll show you the boat.'

Angus and Ryno turned towards the racks, the rest of the paddlers surprised and vaguely disgruntled at the result. They were hoping for more fireworks.

Angus hauled out the tired old Nalon K1 single canoe. It was broken – missing a cockpit and suffering from general overuse and neglect. But he reckoned it would suffice.

'*Yussie, meneer, is jy seker?*' asked Ryno. '*My eie boot!*'

'I didn't say you could have it. I said you could borrow it. But if you keep coming back and you improve, then we'll find you a better one to borrow. Make no mistake, this is a tough sport. It's not for sissies.'

'I'm not scared, *meneer.*'

'I'm not your *meneer*. I'm Angus. Now come. Enough buggering around. Let's see you on the water. Can you balance yet?'

Angus was pretty sure that the little kid would wobble out onto the dam and fall out of his boat. Ryno dragged the boat across the grass.

'*Wat van 'n sitplek, meneer?*'

'You can have a seat if you can balance. And it's "Angus".'

'*Ek's* Ryno.'

The youngster took his time. He had chutzpah, even Angus had to give him that. Then he nestled himself gently into the boat and pushed himself off from the bank.

'Aren't you missing something?' Angus shook his head, 'Like maybe a paddle?'

'We just use our hands, Angus!'

Ryno wobbled off towards the middle of the dam, pushing his hands through the cool water.

The Discovery of Power Park

Ten years later, Ryno sits in the passenger seat of a D5 Land Rover, headed down the Old Potchefstroom Road on the outskirts of Soweto. It will be several years before South Africa holds the Soccer World Cup and the area is tidied up for the tourists. Baragwanath Hospital passes to the left – grey, stoic and weighed down by inefficiency and backlogs – and the large taxi rank to the right – informal, vibrant and bustling. It is said that you can buy anything at the taxi rank, from a ride to the northern suburbs to a vulture's head.

'It's like a carnival at these taxi ranks,' Ryno chuckles.

'The okes run whole businesses in there,' smiles Jacques Theron.

The two couldn't be more different – Jacques, a tall, strongly built *boer seun* from a dairy-and-fruit farm near Barrydale, and Ryno, short, stocky and full of the laughter he learned in his home town near Stellenbosch.

'So there's a dam down here on the right,' he says. 'We drove past it the other day.'

'Okay, *kom ons gaan kyk.*'

Minutes later, the sponsor-branded Land Rover turns right into the suburb of Power Park. It winds its way down the potholed roads in the general direction of Orlando Dam. The houses there, built for white government employees, stand as reminders of a brutal bygone era – but the current occupants can be seen watering their geraniums and marigolds in the light of a late Friday afternoon.

The Land Rover approaches the water's edge. Aside from a discarded orange tobacco packet and a few broken pieces of brown glass, the lake looks clear and seems clean – a good start.

'*Hy's perfek,*' Jacques says, surveying the water.

'The guys can paddle here no problem,' agrees Ryno.

'*Nou soek ons net 'n paar roeiers.*'

'Ja, we need paddlers that can already swim.'

The enormity of the task does not escape either of the young men as they stand on the bank. Forming a club to develop the sport in under-privileged communities will not be easy – this much they already know.

When they are driving away through the streets again, the sound of water splashing catches Ryno's attention. Splashing water – and children playing.

'Hey, man, turn off the car!'

'What?'

'Turn off the car. It's kids playing in a swimming pool.'

'Oh. Ja. So …?

'It sounds like swimming lessons.'

Finally, Jacques understands.

'Good point. We could be in the money here.'

He pulls over to the pavement and stops the car.

Moments later, the pair are walking into a beautifully maintained public swimming pool, filled with the lively banter of children. A tall, lean young man approaches them – Mike Sigwile. Over the next few years, Mike Sigwile will play a crucial role in the development of the Soweto Canoe and Recreation Club. He is already a well-regarded swimming coach in Power Park.

Within weeks, Jacques and Ryno have included games in stable plastic canoes as part of Mike's weekly lessons. A handful of local kids from the nearby communities establish themselves as regular and enthusiastic participants in these sessions. As they become competent at the sport, this core group gradually migrates to the Orlando Dam, taking on the challenges of much narrower fibreglass racing boats. Gradually, they will tell their friends about the fun to be had through this strange new sport. Some of these children come from the more formal brick houses in Power Park, but more of them come from the surrounding informal settlements such as Elias Motsoaledi – where the houses are built from pieces of corrugated iron and other found materials.

Many children are soon joining the canoe club – excited by the prospect of acquiring a new skill, the availability of the intriguing equipment and the diversion from their lives in the informal settlements. They learn how to swim and eventually graduate to paddling K1s and K2s on the Orlando Dam. Once they reach a certain level of competence, however, their interest often wanes as the challenges of progressing further in the sport dawn on them. Ryno is quick to pick up on this tendency, though. Inspired by the fact that travel agents seem to promote white-water rafting with great success, he believes that the secret to the long-term success of the club is to introduce the kids to paddling on the rivers on the weekends.

His initiatives are not without their challenges, however. Taking a group of children who did not grow up with swimming pools and teaching them these skills is a big step. The enthusiasm of a new canoeist must survive several months of falling into cold water and they must develop core-stabilising muscles and a sense of balance different from that required by any other sport.

Even in communities where there is an awareness of canoeing, it is not a sport in which children automatically or traditionally take part. The final step of moving from the dam to actually participating in competitive events around the country requires the development of an additional set of skills – such as reading the current in moving water and negotiating rapids – which, in many cases, can be dangerous. Even the smallest obstacle, such as a fallen tree or a man-made weir, when approached incorrectly, can result in a smashed boat and a bruised and battered body. Through mis-judgement, lack of concentration or sometimes just bad luck, even the most experienced, competent and competitive canoeists can suffer a mishap that will end their race on a river. Against the backdrop of these challenges, Ryno sets his sights on building the club – and he never flinches.

Slaying Giants

The years of paddling and teaching in my mid- to late-twenties are glory years for me. The sport of paddling completely absorbs me. I live my dream, paddling for my country and competing – always near the top of the sport locally. After the World Championships in Hungary, I join Colin Simpkins in Canada, where we paddle across the St Lawrence Seaway against an international field to win the Grand Traverse World Sea Kayak Championships. It's an incredible adventure.

In 2000, the year after Hungary, I compete in a World Cup event in Stockton, England. Halfway through the race, I claw my way up to the front group and paddle on the wave of the five-time world champion, Ivan Lawler. I'm ecstatic to finish eighth and it's just as well because it's as good a result as I'll get. In Canada, Spain, England, Denmark and the Czech Republic, I fly the flag. I'm not fast enough to compete with the very best, but I'm content. Back home, I win the Fish River Marathon with Graham Bird. After two days of racing against fellow South African team crew, Russell Willis and Jacques Theron, and the legendary combination of Robbie Herreveld and Graham Monteith – multiple winners themselves – three boats crash into each other over the final 3-metre weir in Cradock. We are the dominant boat, though, and fortunately we come out on top to win my first 'Grand Prix' event.

It's also during these years that the sport is revolutionised in South

Africa. A group of younger, more talented and more focused paddlers, led by Len Jenkins, Ant Stott, Hank McGregor and, later, Shaun Rubenstein, take the sport to a new level. While we made the South African team and competed with mediocre results overseas, they take on the world's best and win medals.

In 2004, the year I'll turn thirty, things start to change for me. Shelley finishes studying Medicine after seven years and finally she feels set free – and we decide to travel. We choose Australia as a base – where we can earn Aussie dollars and travel to countries we've yet even to hear of. And the sun shines. I had tried teaching and living in London some years before that, and the grey drizzle nearly killed me. We spend two incredible years living in Northern Queensland and Sydney, and we travel through New Zealand and Southeast Asia. It's a wonderful life. The local paddling scene back in South Africa had started to get a little monotonous for me and the break does me good. I paddle on the rivers and in the sea. Surf-ski paddling is a new challenge and revitalises my love of paddling. Towards the end of our time there, I find myself paddling out on Sydney harbour with Brad one afternoon.

In less than an hour, the sun will set behind the Opera House. The sunlight glints on the wavelets as we hug the eastern shoreline. We're tiny in the harbour, two surf-ski paddlers with the city sprawling behind us and the rocky cliffs towering to our right.

'As far as big cities go, Sydney must be one of the most beautiful,' I shout to Brad.

'It sure is,' he replies. Then, after a pause, 'Spectacular. Think of those other guys, sitting in the traffic. Or even taking the ferry – it's not the same as being here – right on the water.'

'Keeps us sane.'

Our paddles catch the water in unison for a moment and then the cadences vary once more. We turn our backs on Shark Island to the west and head towards the rocky promontory of South Head.

Sydney harbour is one of the most protected natural harbours in the world. As a paddler, one moment you're cruising happily, with Watson's Bay off to your right, the next you round South Head to find yourself buffeted by the full extent of the moody South Pacific Ocean. The swell is perfect for us on this evening, though – we may be experienced paddlers, but we're near novices in the sea. We turn back towards the city, catch the run and enjoy the wave-ride as long as we can, squeezing out the power of the swell, almost until it disappears. Then we go back for another, despite the setting sun, and then another – just because we can.

Heading back west, watching the sunset, we settle into an easy rhythm.

'How're you feeling about Oz?' I probe.

Brad's been in Sydney now for eighteen months – toughing it out for a passport, I reckon. For Shelley and me, it's different. We're only on a mission to save dollars and travel.

'Struggling. I miss home.'

'How can you miss home? Paddling at the duck pond doesn't quite compare to this!'

I stop paddling for a moment to gesture towards the setting sun behind the harbour. I know what he's thinking, but I'm just putting the bait out. And he knows it. That's the good humour of old-time friends.

'You know. It's the old friends you've built up. And extended family.'

'I know what you mean.'

'But it's also something else. The challenges are tangible back home.'

He lets the point sink in for a while. The sea breeze is still warm, even though we're approaching autumn.

'If you drive home from work here, you don't see any beggars on the corner. But it doesn't mean they're not still standing on the side of the road, thousands of kilometres away in Jo'burg.'

Now he's getting to the point. And it's what I want to hear. So I chip in:

'Alan talks about giants.'

'What's that?'

'Alan Storey.'

'Ja?'

'He talks about slaying giants. He makes an analogy between the challenges we face every day and how pertinent they seem – and living in a land of giants.'

'Makes sense.'

'Anyone can feel like a grasshopper in the face of giants. But if you can stay in the land of giants, you have the opportunity to slay them. It really means something. Back in SA, the giants are right in front of you.'

'Ja. Even I had more of a sense of purpose there. I could feel like I was really making a difference to people. Somehow, the challenges are more tangible.'

'Exactly.'

The sun has long since gone below the horizon. The last pink, wispy clouds above us will soon fade as the deep blue engulfs them, ushering in the stars.

Later, we're changing at the back of Brad's car – a post-paddling ritual. A young man approaches us.

'You rich Rose Bay guys think you can park anywhere!'

He seems half aggressive. Or maybe just annoyed. I can't exactly place his accent. Eastern European, I think.

'I'm not from Rose Bay,' Brad starts.

My old mate has that physical solidarity about him, which, when reinforced by his self-confidence, means not many people would choose to pick a fight with him. When we arrived earlier, I knew we were parking in the parking space too early, but usually after around 5.30pm nobody needs to get into the parking lot. Besides, who can possibly read all the small print in the Sydney by-laws? I always think. Just when you think you've got it right, there's a detail you've missed. It's always: 'No parking on weekdays between 06h00 and 18h00, on weekends and public holidays between 09h00 and 13h00.' That's fine, but then it's a '60 degree angle parking to the kerb only' and 'car share vehicles only'. We might have shared the car but do we need to be authorised as a car-pool vehicle? Is there a sticker we're supposed to put on the windscreen? There are so many rules, it's impossible to keep track.

'Sorry, I'll be out of your way in a moment. I didn't think anyone would be coming in here so late,' Brad continues. I'm impressed – Brad at his most diplomatic.

'I work in the offices – clean them at night,' our fellow immigrant continues.

'Okay, fair enough – sorry. We'll be out in a sec.'

'It's illegal, you know,' he carries on.

I start to worry. Brad has already said he'll move.

'Hey, I said I'll move.'

'Oh, so you're South African?'

'What difference does it make? I'll move now.'

'Don't try and treat me like a black guy.'

This catches me by surprise, so I pipe up:

'What?' I feel the hairs stand up on my neck, my stomach tightens. A 'this guy's asking for it and I'm scared Brad's gonna give it to him' type of feeling is creeping up on me.

'You South Africans are so arrogant. You just want to push everyone around. Just like the black guys at home.'

'What's that got to do with anything?' Brad's getting annoyed, too. He stands up, swinging his legs off the tailgate of his car and, suddenly, our Eastern European friend is bolting towards his car behind me. I turn and, completely out of character, swing the door shut before he can climb in. Not aggressively, just 'economy of motion' is what I'm thinking. Besides, I think, he's started an argument and the debate's not over.

'Hey,' he shouts. 'Hey! You make a big mistake now!'

Brad chuckles threateningly.

'Do me a favour – don't insult us. We'll be out of your way in a moment.'

Silence.

Then, slowly, the other guy opens his door, climbs in and closes it again.

We finish packing up quietly while our Eastern European friend sits sulking in his van. As we climb into the Land Cruiser and head out into the darkening street, I wonder briefly what his story is. Is he here on his own? With his family? They say big cities can be the loneliest of places, and as we drive home in our little cocoon, while the big city hums, I can believe it.

One thing I'll certainly miss about living in Sydney is paddling in the ocean. The sea is so changeable and so much more fun. I stand chatting to Brad on the beach, an early Saturday-morning pleasure. We're at Rose Bay after the time trial. Tommy Woodriff, the archetypal surfing life-saver – big, tough and good-looking – is strutting along the beach towards us, having just won the Rose Bay time trial. Tommy was born to be on the sea. He has an uncanny ability to read the waves and use them to his advantage – propelling his surf-ski forward like a missile while others are still scratching around, looking for the tiniest wave-run. For us Jo'burg boys, born and bred in the big city, 6 000 kilometres from the coastline, it's exceedingly frustrating. We just don't have the same feel for the ocean.

'I really want to get that thing running,' Brad is saying. He's talking about the Soweto canoe club back home. Jacques and Ryno have given it the initial push but it's in need of more energy and funds to ensure its survival. Brad wants to head back to South Africa in order to do it – and I wouldn't bet against him.

'Ah, mate, we'll really miss you if you do,' Tommy joins in.

'It's a giant worth slaying,' Brad replies.

I just smile.

Good Times

In September of 2006, Shelley and I are married under a cherry-blossom tree in the garden of her family home in Westcliff, Johannesburg. It's a beautiful day and she's a beautiful bride. Alan Storey conducts the ceremony in front of a crowd of over a hundred people. The fact that he's a special friend makes the evening even more meaningful. We settle in Parkview, buying the oldest, cheapest house in the best street we can afford. It's a ramshackle disaster of a place with peeling ceilings and leaking gutters, but we hardly notice. It has soul. And character. And we're happy together.

During this time, I form a great paddling partnership with three-time Berg winner, Jacques Theron. Like me, Jacques is 'old school' in many ways and fits the expression, *'Hy vat nie kak van kaboutetjies nie'*. His relaxed demeanour in the boat is great for me. In my early years, I could become overly tense and intense before races, but Jacques soon knocks that out of my approach. Together, we're able to dominate the Gauteng scene, but we come second in race after race on the national stage. For two years, there's always just one boat faster than us in every major race. We've finished on the podium in more than ten of the country's major races when, eventually, we 'out-tough' the competition to win the Breede Canoe Marathon.

In 2008, our daughter Emma is born. It's a great day. I drive slower on the way home from the hospital than I've ever driven before. I'm incredulous at the other drivers, who seem oblivious to the value of my cargo. I'm also aware of the shift in perspective that I'm required to make with regard to my paddling. Then, a week later, I'm surprised by what happens. I leave work early and am astonished at my own mindset: I was preparing to make the sacrifice of not going to the dam to train but to head home to see Shelley and Emma, but that's not how it happens: I *want* to go home, not to the dam to train.

Jacques and I keep paddling well, though. We win the Vaal and go on to win the Umkomaas too, in a controversial clash with Hank McGregor and Grant van der Walt through the last rapid of the race. It's a great partnership, which eventually leads to my conducting the wedding ceremony for Jacques and his wife Jen – an Olympic paddler herself. It's a request I'll treasure for years to come. The truth is, our combination is easy because communicating is easy. Jacques and I speak Afrikaans until things need to happen in a hurry in the boat and then we switch smartly to English! But we race the same way. I sometimes know before he pushes the pedals which way he's going to manoeuvre around the bunch. Nothing is ever a hassle with Jacques.

Classroom Visit

There's a knock at the door. I turn away from the class and open it. To my surprise, a deputy head-girl from two years before, Dayle Malherbe, walks into my classroom.

'Hello, Mr Cruickshanks.'

'Hi, Dayle.' I'm taken aback but delighted at the visit from a past pupil. Teachers always are. 'How're you doing?'

'Very well thanks, and you?' The formalities of the pupil-teacher relationship are still entrenched.

'Well. To what do we owe this visit?'

I'm just thinking that things are somewhat awkward in front of the class of girls in front of me. Being Grade 11s, they'll all remember her well from two years earlier. But Dayle takes over.

'Hi, guys,' she smiles.

They look at her, appreciative of the distraction, intrigued by ideas of varsity, first year, orientation and freedom – concepts that they know she has an infinitely greater understanding of despite being only eighteen months away from leaving school themselves. Eighteen months seems nothing in my frame of reference but an infinite lifetime in theirs.

'I just wanted to share the most important lesson I learned in this classroom.'

'Okay,' I interject, nervously. 'I mean, is it appropriate?'

'How could it not be?'

'Fair enough,' I smile, shaking my head, 'go ahead.'

So she does. 'When I was in Grade 10,' she begins, 'Mr Cruickshanks threw my Jane Austen study guide out of the window.'

'What?'

I don't immediately remember, but it sounds like something I might have done.

'You did.'

The class laughs. I frown.

'That doesn't sound right.'

And then I remember actually doing it – but not why.

'So, Mr Cruickshanks threw my study guide for *Pride and Prejudice* out of the window because he thought that I should be developing my own ideas rather than reading from a study guide that was trying to tell me what to think.'

Then it all comes back to me. Dayle was *dux* scholar material. She was brilliant – almost a model student, in fact. She worked hard, put it all out there. And she had that thirst for knowledge that won't accept anything less than a full, clear explanation from the teacher. 'Almost' a model student because she needed to back her own opinions more. She knew all the right answers, sometimes instinctively, but she didn't always 'know she knew'. Mathematics was different – there she completely creamed it: 100% was only just enough for her in Maths.

I have always encouraged my pupils to develop and trust their own ideas around literature and texts. One day, more than likely last lesson on a Friday when English lessons can be particularly sleepy, I'd seen a study guide on Dayle's desk. As a demonstration of my disapproval, I'd taken it and thrown it out of the window of our first-floor classroom. It was, no doubt, a moment of minor recklessness. Clearly, she remembered though.

'Oh,' I say quietly at the expectant class, 'maybe I did.'

There's some laughter from the girls who think I should be embarrassed but not too much.

'And thank you for that lesson,' Dayle says. 'I remember it.'

I'm still a bit embarrassed but then the bell rings. Saved by the old adage. I chat to Dayle for a while. She is on the Dean's list. She won the prize for the top Accounting student at Wits at the end of the previous year. Wow. There are few things more rewarding than seeing the success of a past pupil and knowing that you might have had a part in that – no matter how small.

After she has left, I sit on the edge of my desk, staring at the bare tree outside the window with my legs swinging. I think about the many pupils I've taught, the mistakes I've made and the successes they've had. Sometimes, I think that the most impact one can hope to make is with the weaker pupils. They need more from you. And I start to think about what it means to be a teacher. Yes, Dayle Malherbe did come back to visit. In a way, they do sometimes thank you. Earlier that year, I'd asked a senior class how many of them planned on starting their careers in South Africa. Less than half of them raised their hands. I wanted to educate citizens of the world. I wanted to create a global awareness. But is this what slaying giants is all about?

At Home in the Valley of a Thousand Hills

I lie back on my towel, allowing the aftermath of eight hours of paddling and running to settle into my bones. The non-stop Dusi is a different type of challenge. The race takes all day. The sun can be pitiless, the heat relentless. God, it's a tough race. I've had some hard days out there some years. I've finished second twice and third twice. But this time I lie under the marquee in the knowledge that this – this is my day.

'*Mfowethu*, where are you going now?'

It's a source of great pride that Thulani Mbanjwa, the first black winner of the Dusi, still calls me '*mfowethu*'. We've spent our toughest day together and this time we've come out on top – at last.

'I'm not too sure. It feels like a long way back home tonight.'

The road back to Johannesburg seems preposterous right now. I can think of nothing worse than getting into my car after the prize-giving and driving for six hours. I've been ignoring the issue, though, and savouring the win while we wait for the prize-giving.

'What are you doing?' I ask.

'I'm going home.' He pauses. 'Why don't you just stay at my place?'

The thought intrigues me. The magnificent valley dotted with little white huts. I've paddled through the valley and run through it hundreds of times in races and in training. It would certainly be a different experience.

'Are you sure?'

'Of course, *mfowethu*. I'd love you to stay at my house.'

I reckon 'Bungy', as he's called, has the biggest grin in the country. He's a home-grown talent in every sense. He's from the valley and still lives in the valley. Tall and strongly built, I reckon Shaka would be proud – Thulani's a warrior of note.

'Okay, cool.' I can't hide the excitement in my face.

I relax again and think about the day that's been. The start at Camps Drift at first light this morning seems years ago. This is going to go down as a day of memories, that's for sure. A while later a familiar hand wraps around mine. I open my eyes and look up: Shelley.

'Hey!'

'Surprise!'

I'm in shock. I can't quite believe she's here.

'Well done, my love.'

Shelley explains how, when she heard we were leading the race, she bought herself a plane ticket and got herself to the prize-giving.

Later that evening, Shelley and I are greeted like old friends outside a small brick building by Thulani's family. At that time, he lives on a hill overlooking 'Table Mountain' above the Umsindusi and Umgeni valleys. It's the sort of view that makes you want to just sit and watch the passing of rural life on the slopes below. In 30 seconds, I've exhausted my entire isiZulu vocabulary. His mother has exhausted her only English word – 'Hello'. We sit at the table eating chicken and pap. My body is desperate – it seems to crave the protein ... and the fat. Tim Noakes would nod, knowingly. Thulani and I laugh about the race. We recount how we 'broke' our nearest competitors mentally when we matched them on the Guinea Fowl portage.

'*Masihambe, mfowethu!*' – 'Let's go, brother,' he'd shouted. Using one of the few isiZulu phrases I understood to inspire me at the critical moment. They would have expected to be the stronger runners, we the stronger paddlers. When we stayed with them on the run, their spirits must have sunk. That day, I paddled the Dusi as well as I'd ever paddled a river. I don't think I made a single mistake. Thulani's extraordinary power had pushed me along on the running sections and we'd combined beautifully in the paddling. Now we joked about running over Burma Road portage at the end of a long day, though it had been no joke at the time, that's for sure. The river had been low – the kind where the warm, stagnant pools seem to offer little encouragement – and we'd been sitting on a four-minute cushion for a lead, so we'd had nothing to gain by taking the risk in paddling around. We also knew what the win would mean to each of us – and so we'd run. We'd taken the boat out and thrown it on our shoulders for the toughest portage of the day in the midday heat and the full humidity of the valley.

Soon enough, the rest of our company are bored of listening to a conversation they either can't understand or have grown tired of. I always feel for the friends and family – because paddlers can talk! We can regale each other with stories to the point where they seem to take on a life of their own – perhaps even worse than fishermen.

'Okay, should we grab a mattress?' I ask Thulani.

He smiles and stands. 'I'll show you and Shelley to your room.'

'*Siyabonga*,' we say to his mother. She just smiles. Then, to our surprise, Thulani takes us out of the house and to the door of a small traditional hut a few metres away.

'You'll be staying in my room tonight,' he laughs.

'Really? You're sure?' is all we can manage.

He opens the door and sets a paraffin lamp on the floor, turns and walks back to the house. We look inside. The room is perfectly round and dominated by a queen-size bed directly opposite us. It's backed by a magnificent, ornate headboard and adorned with a silky maroon bedspread. We're completely taken aback and astonished by Thulani's generosity. We lie back on the bed and marvel at it all. Here, in the middle of rural KwaZulu-Natal, we lie in a white-washed hut with a corrugated-iron roof – but it's not all rural, not by a long shot. There's an enormous flat-screen TV and a sound system with surround sound. I reckon it'd be a muso's dream. For now, it's our dream.

We wake the next morning, looking up at a corrugated-iron roof with tiny shards of light poking through tiny rows of holes. Thulani assures me later that it doesn't leak. How the light bounces through then, I'm not too sure. We lie there, listening to cocks crowing and the odd shout down the valley – and sometimes the bark of a dog. My body aches. Everywhere. Yet I have never felt so satisfied.

Eventually, there's a knock at the door. Thulani's mother brings in a large plastic basin of water collected by her and warmed on the primus stove. There's also a bar of soap, still covered in its pink-and-white wrapping.

'*Siyabonga*, Mama.'

She lays the basin and soap down on the floor in front of us, nods, smiles and leaves the room. This is room service of a different kind. An unexpected gesture that might not be the luxury of a five-star establishment but one that leaves us feeling deeply privileged and grateful. My need for connection and meaning in South Africa has been completely answered. It's a memory Shelley and I will treasure for the rest of our lives.

Pressure Cooker

'I just can't go on like this any more, Steve.'

'So is this what you really want?'

'Have you done anything? Been to see anyone?'

'I don't know if I can do it like that.'

The two characters look at each other, full of tears. They're beating themselves up. Steve can't face what happened – what he thinks he's done. He can't forgive himself. Instead, he drives himself. Punishes himself physically by running and paddling. It's his way of dealing with it – and of not dealing with it.

As for Annie, she forgave him long ago. She never blamed him in the first place. She's dealt with the loss of their child. But, with that, she also lost her husband. She stares at him. Somewhere in there, he's also lost himself.

I watch the film. It works. I have to give that to Craig and Robbie. I think it's great. But it's not our story. Shelley isn't Annie. And I might be a pain in the ass, as Duma tells Steve, but I'm not Steve.

•

I've been training late again. I'm driving home from the dam in the dark. One thing you have to realise is that competing close to the top of a sport – and I never quite made the very top, even nationally – absorbs an inordinate amount of energy and time. Mostly, it's the time that gets you in the end. I pull up the driveway a good half an hour later than I'd hoped. It's already been dark for a while.

Shelley's been cooking. Mostly, she's a terrible cook – so I guess that's why I generally do the cooking. It's a pretty good arrangement – she's far happier clearing up the pots. And she's a whole lot better than I am at earning a living too. But it's been a long day. I was at the gym at 5am, then teaching all day, then at the dam for a hard training session in the evening. But she's not impressed. Somehow, we get into an argument about priorities and canoeing training and work and the difference between recreational fitness and competitive sport. And what's going to happen when our first child arrives? Shelley's pregnant. I'm too tired to bother about the details or even to follow the logic of the argument eventually. I have an inkling that I'm being stubborn but I still want to compete and that's that. Before I know it, Shelley's thrown a piece of – in my opinion – over-cooked hake at me and it hits me in the chest.

'It's delicious!' she informs me.

So I sit outside on the step of our patio, taking small bites of a piece of cold hake. It's a beautiful late summer's evening and the plane tree sways above me in the warm breeze. It's not that I feel I can't paddle as fast as I used to. I think I probably can. But I know that the guys at the top are doing this canoeing thing more professionally than me. They have more time to train – they make more time to train – and then more time to rest and recover between sessions. Not only that, they're better in the first place – either they started the sport younger or their genetic seeding is superior. I'm past 35 and I actually want to spend more time on my career. I love the sport but I also love education. I'm not only in love with my wife, I have a sense that when our child is born there might be some tough decisions to make.

PART 3

Dangwani to Johannesburg

The five-year-old boy looks out of the window of the minibus. The valleys, mountains and rivers are familiar. Not the same, but similar to the valley they have left in darkness early that morning. They seem to pass mountains and more mountains, valleys and more valleys. The world seems so big. He is too naïve to understand how different the world he is approaching will be from the world he has known. The world he is leaving behind is one where little boys are expected to splash at the edge of rivers when the midday sun becomes too hot; they are expected to climb trees and play with stones and branches and not stray too far from the house and the village of Dangwani. As long as he was 'in sight of' the village, his mother would be happy and would not lambast him and his friends. As long as he and his sister remembered to collect wood and complete their chores before dark, his mother would smile and all would be well when he went to bed that night. 'In sight of' the village meant he could be a kilometre away in some directions.

The busyness of Mthatha, where they'd changed buses in the early light, had excited him.

'Mama, is this the town we are going to?' he asked.

'Johannesburg is still far,' she replied.

He would find out soon enough that the area where he would be able to play in Elias Motsoaledi – the informal settlement he and his family were headed – would be less than 100 square metres. The people living in that street would outnumber the entire village of Dangwani.

They pass many towns that day. After Mthatha, they are soon in Pietermaritzburg, where his mother assures him that Johannesburg is even bigger than the strange city they are passing through. After that, the road becomes wider and there are more cars than he has ever seen. The mountains change from rolling green hills to steep, rocky, flat-topped cliffs and he grows tired and sleeps for a while on his mother's shoulder. When he wakes up, the bus is still going. There are no hills or valleys, the world is just flat and the sun sinks behind fields of mealies, which seem to go all the way to the horizon. A comfortable darkness soon envelops the minibus. After a while, more and more lights appear in the distance and soon there are tall buildings on all sides of them and the bus slows.

'This is the city of Johannesburg,' his mother tells him. The boy looks out the window and is amazed by it all. When the bus finally stops and the people climb out, there are many people walking up and down the pavement and so many cars and buses in the road that he grips tightly to his mother's dress. Again, they change minibuses and his mother tells him that they will soon be with his father. It has been such a long day that he can barely keep his eyes open as they pass through streets, where there are tiny houses built so closely together that there is barely any space between them. When the second minibus eventually stops in one of these streets, his mother has to wake him up again. Later that night, in the darkness of this unfamiliar place, Siseko lies awake, listening to the sounds of his new home.

Township Life

It seems to Siseko that the new life is better. He is only five and he can barely remember the days before his father came to Johannesburg. But now at least the family is all together. Most evenings, when his father comes home, he brings sweets. And they have a stove now. There's no need to collect wood and it's easier for his mother to cook. Admittedly, there are hassles too. They live in a rented shack on the property of Mr Mokala's house. It's much smaller than the old mud-and-brick house near Dingwani and Mr Mokala won't allow children to run around or make a noise in the yard, but he's out a lot of the time – and kids are quick to learn the tricks.

Siseko starts school and, within two years, they move to a slightly larger shack. It's still a shack, though. The floor is smoothly swept earth in places. Although he hears his father commenting that money is hard to come by, there is always food to eat. If his mother sends him to buy bread for lunch, he soon learns to keep going from spaza shop to spaza shop to find Blue Ribbon – because with this bread there are twenty slices rather than the eighteen of Albany. When he gets home, five slices will be for Tata, five for Mama, five for Lusanda and then he can have three and leave two for Simnikiwe. Also, they have hot water from the stove to wash. Not everyone has hot water.

At Christmas time, his mother takes him, Lusanda and Simnikiwe to town. Early in the morning, his father is back from his last night shift for the year and he lights the stove and cooks pap for the family. When they wake, he gives some money to Mama. The older children are excited about this annual ritual. After breakfast, they walk to the taxi rank. It is already warm and the highveld sun is well above the horizon, even though it is only half past six. The air is clearer in summer without the lighting of so many fires.

'Where are we going?' Simnikiwe asks. He is too young to have been on the previous year's trip.

'We're going to town,' Siseko informs him, 'to buy new clothes.'

Simnikiwe is also too young to remember that he has been on a taxi before. It seems like a great adventure to him. As they get into town, there is more traffic and it moves slowly, the driver surges into gaps between other cars and the other drivers hoot. Simnikiwe cheers because to him it's like a race. Siseko and Lusanda smile but Mama just frowns. Eventually, they arrive at the big taxi rank in town and they climb out of the minibus. When they get to Eloff Street, there are already hawkers trying to sell food and other goods on the pavement. There is an extraordinary busyness that they have never experienced before. But it's also the glory years – the Madiba years of the Rainbow Nation – and, unbeknown to Siseko and his siblings, the economy is taking off. Simnikiwe stops to try on a pair of Ray-Ban sunglasses, but his mother quickly reprimands him: 'We haven't got money for those.'

'They're imitation anyway,' Lusanda tells him, and they carry on walking. They go into Pep stores, where Siseko tries on a red-and-blue-checked, long-sleeved shirt. They all agree that it suits him but then his mother looks closely at the stitching and is not impressed with the quality. She vetoes the shirt and they move on. Siseko is annoyed.

'You'll be grateful later on,' she tells him. 'That shirt wouldn't have lasted long.'

He knows that they don't go shopping often and so he accepts her point. Besides, he has learned that there are times when it's not worth it to argue. By midday, they are all tired of walking and their mother buys them bunny chow from a vendor on the corner of Fox Street and the children sit on the bottom step of the entrance to a building to eat. Simnikiwe keeps checking to make sure that Siseko still has the bag with his two new shirts and jeans in it. Lusanda asks who CCMA is and why he needs such a big house. When their mother says that she has no idea what she's talking about, she points to a big blue sign that says, 'CCMA House', but still this doesn't help.

'Maybe it's the name of a company,' Mama tells her.

After they have eaten, they return to the taxi rank and catch a taxi back to Soweto. By the time they have walked back to Elias, it is mid-afternoon. But there's still time to play and Siseko and Simnikiwe go to see if they can find some of the other kids. As they walk down the road, Siseko thinks that the world couldn't really be much better.

Being Good at Something

Siseko wakes early one Friday morning. They are still in the shack but over the years many more have been built up around them. It is dark inside but his father has the water boiling. He hears his son shuffling under the blanket. He pulls the curtain to the side to see his three children lying on the mattresses.

'The candle's burned out.'

'Sorry, Tata. I had to finish my Maths homework. And it took some time.'

'Mama and Simnikiwe were finished by eight.'

'Sorry. The work is more difficult in Grade 10.'

'Sure. You must keep doing your best, my son. We'll have to start next week's candle.'

'After school, I can go to Auntie Maria to ask if she has spare.'

'Okay.'

Siseko lies in the half-darkness while his father quietly goes about the business of dressing and preparing for work. Once his father has left and the shack is motionless again, he lies for a long time, listening to the cocks crowing and the distant traffic. These precious moments to himself are interrupted now and then by the voices of people already in the street on their way to work. After some time, he hears his mother moving around and starting to make porridge. At 6am, he wakes his brother and they start to dress for school.

Later, Siseko and Simnikiwe walk toward the school carrying their school bags. At the bus shelter, some of the boys are already smoking. One of them laughs and waves at Siseko.

'Still living the clean life!' he shouts.

'*Eita*, my *bra*!' Siseko laughs.

'Sure.'

Although many of the boys at Thaba Jabula Secondary School are bigger than Siseko, he has discovered that very few of them can run as fast as he knows he can. Throughout the morning, he struggles to concentrate in class because he knows that today is going to be a good day. Today, they will run against many boys from other schools. The teacher has said that they are going to a new place – Zoo Lake – to run.

After school, he joins the other boys and girls in the dusty parking area in front of the school gates. The bus takes them onto the highway and past the city buildings that he has seen only on the few occasions when he has gone with his mother to buy clothes at the shops in the city. It is fun to be away from school for the day. Many of the boys and girls run because of the outing and the fun in the bus on the way there and back, but for Siseko it is different. Sure, those things are fun, and his mother always packs him some lunch from home for these days, which is nicer than the bunny chow he usually buys from the parents who set up a stall at break-time on the field next to the school. But there's something else. He loves the feeling of being good at something. It prides him to know that he is faster than the others. Not only that, near the end when he's tired, when they are all tired, he knows that they will all give up before him. He is stronger than them and that means something. He is like his father: tougher than the rest.

When the bus turns off the highway, they join a road that snakes down a steep hill past the big houses and office buildings. Near the bottom, Mr Masinga tells them that the zoo is on their right and all of the younger boys crane their necks, trying to see if they can see a lion, or at least a giraffe. The older boys look nonchalantly at all of this because it is not their first time on a running outing and it is important that the others

71

know that they have seen it all before. Before they have had a proper chance to look, however, the bus turns away from the zoo and into a potholed parking lot, where it slots in alongside the other buses. By now, the children are all laughing and chattering with excitement.

Later, Siseko lines up just behind the red-and-white tape. His old friend from Pimville Primary days – Sipho – greets him with a grin. 'Don't start too fast. You'll get tired before the end,' he laughs, 'and then Sifiso will beat you – like always!'

'Sharp. Good to see you,' Siseko smiles. If only you knew, he thinks.

This is the part that he loves. He just has a moment to think, this is what I'm good at. Then the gun fires and they're all running. Along the avenue of trees, the young boys sprint. Siseko is worried because the boys in front seem to be going much faster than he knows he can run for the 3-kilometre route. The shortly cropped grass is so comfortable to run on compared to the dust and gravel of the course at Thaba Jabula, though. They turn left at the end of the line of trees and follow the tape down into a dip. A much longer line of runners follows behind him. Good. Not so bad, he thinks.

The acorns hurt his feet as they run under the dappled shade of the big oak tree and he has to slow his pace to make the hard right turn. Then they snake along the path next to the lake. His breathing is loud and heavy, his chest burns. Already, the bunch of boys at the front has thinned out. Now there are about five at the front and then a strung out-line, falling off the pace. That's good news because some of them are getting tired and coming back to him. By the time they reach the restaurant at the far end of the lake, there are only four boys in front of him. His lungs still burn and his breathing is fast.

As they turn, to start up the hill, the white vest of a boy in front of him, whom he doesn't know, is immediately closer. Good – he doesn't like the uphills, Siseko thinks. He leans into the hill, pumping his arms, and passes the boy in the white vest easily. Now there are only three. He looks at Vusi's back. He's found that if he just keeps his eyes on their backs and imagines being tied to them by a rope, he can pull that rope tighter and tighter, drawing himself closer and closer until the gap has gone and he's with them. He breathes and breathes, tightens and tightens the rope, until the gap is smaller and smaller. Then the gap is gone and he's with Vusi. Then he's alongside, then past.

Now there's only Sifiso and another runner he doesn't know, perhaps 20 metres in front of him. They turn right around a lamppost with a piece of red-and-white tape strung from it and race down the hill past the tennis courts. He knows Sifiso loves the downhills and immediately he can see him edging ahead on his own. Moments later, he passes the other boy, who is standing bent over, his hands on his hips.

All the way down the hill, Siseko tries to hang on to Sifiso. He opens his stride, stretches his legs, tries to force himself to run faster. The path meanders to the left and then to the right and eventually they're into the dip at the bottom, passing the square, neatly cut lawns with the old men and women all dressed in white – playing their own game. Siseko knows he's done well because he's only lost a few metres on the long downhill. He wrestles with fatigue, pushing himself further and further out of his comfort zone, until he's right behind Sifiso. Sifiso hears the footfalls and glances back – a look of recognition rather than surprise on his face. It becomes a battle of pride as the two runners race side by side, as they pass the shouting girls who stand waiting to start their race. Cheering voices and excited, beckoning eyes fill their heads as they race past. On and on they run, each refusing to give in. Like Temane and Sinqe, the greatest rivalry of all, thinks Siseko. He pushes the pace faster and faster, hurting himself more and more. Past the basketball courts, the white geese to their right and the lake beyond that – they race. Then they reach a line of stretched red-and-white tape to their left. Both runners are forced to slow their pace as they lean hard to their left and circle a tree. The exposed roots underneath it scrape their feet, but Siseko accelerates away faster. He feels the slight gap and surges. There's no response and he can feel it. He surges again. His legs hurt, he sucks for air. He's ahead. He glances back. There are only about 500 metres to go. He's got it. He's faster, tougher than the rest.

Moments later, however, he stops abruptly. He walks. He watches helplessly as Sifiso goes past him. He walks slowly to the finish line. His friends and some teachers beckon him on. Vusi passes him, chased by the boy in the white vest. In a dazed state, Siseko breaks into a jog and finishes the race fourth. As he puts his hands to his knees, he sees Mr Masinga glowering at him from behind the crowd of excited spectators.

There was a huge celebration on the day of Siseko's birth. A son brings status, continuity and pride to a family living in a rural environment in the Eastern Cape. His father was proud and his mother relieved to have given the family what they so desperately needed. A cow was slaughtered and people came from beyond their valley. Most of the village of Dangwani was there. His mother held her baby with pride and the people saw that it was true – Siseko, son of Zamxolo and Nomazibulo Ntondini, had been born. That rural environment will always be remembered by Siseko for the days playing in the hills and swimming in the rivers. He had little awareness of the hard days at work for his parents.

Many years later, after the move to Johannesburg, when Mrs Moreti at Pimville Primary School asked for a birth certificate for Siseko, there was none. Nor had there ever been one. When he left seven years later for Thaba Jabula, there was still no birth certificate. Finally, when Mr Masinga asked at the school office for copies of the birth certificates for his running team, his heart sank when he saw that Siseko, the young Grade 8 boy with the big smile who ran so fast and with such passion, was one of the ones with no birth certificate. Later, he called him into his classroom.

'Siseko, you can't run in the team because we have no record of your birth.'

When Siseko arrived that afternoon to run – in spite of Mr Masinga's warning – the teacher had explained that if he finished the race in the first three, the officials would ask for his birth certificate. If they did not have one, they would accuse Mr Masinga and Thaba Jabula School of cheating and allowing their pupils to run in the wrong age group.

'But if I don't come in the first three?' Siseko asked.

'If you run, you will come in the first three.'

'But – if I don't?'

'I've seen you run. You will.'

'Please let me run. I promise not to finish in the first three ...'

Since that day, Siseko had run many times in the inter-school races. He had usually finished fourth and sometimes fifth or sixth. More recently, however, he had taken the lead during the first half of the race and then seemed to fade and drop back towards the very end. The problem with the race at Zoo Lake was that it had taken him so long to prove to himself that he could win the race that he had nearly had to stop completely to make sure that three runners still crossed the finish line before him.

Paddling in the Storm

Nkululeko, Ratabele and Siseko walk home together from school. The air is clear and fresh after the heavy rains. The Johannesburg thunderstorms have left the ground soaked and the grass glistens in the late afternoon light. A golden light, shining beneath the still dark clouds.

After school, there are plenty of things to do. They can head for the taxi rank. There's always a lot of excitement there. If you get there soon enough, you can find one of the drivers waiting for passengers for a longer trip – to Diepsloot or, even better, Marabastad. It takes time for these buses to fill up. If you ask nicely, the driver will let you clean their minibus and, if you do a good enough job, there's some money in it. There are also the hawkers on the opposite side of the road – the Baragwanath side. At the end of the day, the fruit and vegetables need to go back to the township. You can find *isalukazi* to give you a little money to help her carry her load. Sometimes she will give you an apple or a banana for your efforts. There was also that time when they stole oranges and ran away with the old granny shouting at them. They'd laughed so hard but then Siseko felt bad afterwards. Most of these things are better done alone, though. The money earned doesn't go very far between three. But it's more fun in a group, so it's always a debate. The three boys are quiet for a while as they walk.

'*Umshado wezinkawu* [a monkeys' wedding],' says Ratabele. Then he has an idea: 'Hey, the river will be racing now.'

'For sure, why don't we paddle it?' Nkululeko picks up on the germinating seed. But he's nervous. 'Eish, remember last time.'

'Ja, Ryno was so cross with us!'

'Yoh! He shouted. And remember the warning!'

'Ja, like an angry bull!'

They walk in silence, remembering the anger of the afternoon when Ryno had discovered they'd been playing in the raging river with no helmets and no life jackets.

Siseko feels out on a limb. He wants to join them but he's never paddled these boats before.

'You know … it's Friday.' Ratabele's not giving up. 'He's never there.'

'Ja, he's probably at a shebeen,' Siseko chimes in and the others laugh, even though they know it's not true. But Siseko's back in the loop and smiling again.

'Let's go past and see.'

'Okay, guys, cheers.' Siseko wants out. He can't join in this adventure.

'No. Come with us, let's just go and see the river,' Ratabele insists.

Minutes later, three pairs of eyes are transfixed by what they see. What is usually a miserable, Lucky-Star-tin and Sunlight-Liquid-infested stream is now a surging river; it's bursting over its banks. A frothy cappuccino foam gathers in the eddy below a neglected mass of concrete. A supermarket trolley rolls casually over and under the water, washed unceremoniously from upstream.

'Yoh.' The three boys stand in awe.

'Are you guys scared?' Siseko asks. He can't paddle anyway so he's just pushing their buttons.

'It's dangerous, man!'

'Ay, I'm not scared. It's just water,' Ratabele shrugs – more bravado than bravery in his tone.

'Come on. I'll watch,' Siseko smiles.

'Ah. You'd also be scared.'

'Me? No chance.'

'Okay, then you come also.'

'I can't even paddle those boats, man. But I wouldn't be scared anyway.'

'Then let's see you swim with that buoyancy thing.'

'What's that?'

'That buoyancy thing. That big polystyrene they put in the boat.'

'Ja, it floats.' Nkululeko joins the fray. Attack is the best form of defence.

'Okay. Sure. I can swim here if you go. But you're not going. You're too scared.'

The three stand in silence for a few moments longer, staring at the river. Contemplating. It looks threatening, properly dangerous. Siseko knows what his mother would say. And his father would give him a hiding to remember if he ever found out.

'I'm going,' Ratabele says, matter of factly, like there'd been no previous discussion at all.

The pendulum's swung. And Nkululeko gives it another shove.

'We all going. Let's go.'

Not long afterwards, the three boys move wordlessly out of the garage and away from the house. Nkululeko and Ratabele with their boats on their shoulders and Siseko begrudgingly behind with the large rectangle of polystyrene under his arm. They jog briskly across the road, out of Power Park and over the fence. Their bare feet squelch along the muddy path.

Standing above the river, looking down at the writhing rapid, Siseko is not scared, just curious. He watches his two friends clumsily climbing into their boats on the grassy banks next to the flow. They edge the noses of their boats towards the current. Ratabele looks back, makes eye contact. There's fear in his eyes. Siseko glances at Nkululeko, his good friend. He sees only excitement and expectation. So he holds the piece of white foam above his head. Then he jumps.

The light's gone. The water's white, then brown, then all is dark. The water tugs at his legs. The polystyrene block seems to try to pull free from his arms, but he holds it tight towards his chest. Then the world is racing past above his head – clouds, long grass, a pylon. His foot touches something hard and he bends his knees up towards himself. Then he hits his shin on something metal. So he swivels his feet behind him and kicks like Mike had shown him that time at the swimming pool. But, mostly, he just grips the polystyrene and hopes for the best.

'Keep your legs up!'

Nkululeko is in the water next to him, shouting, holding the back of the boat. He's obviously fallen out. The current pulls the two of them fast, leaving them with little control over their movements.

They wash over a ledge and into a wider pool. The water is calmer. Then they're all kicking for the bank, laughing in relief and the aftermath of fear and adrenaline. They throw the boats and the white foam onto the bank, still laughing through chattering teeth.

When Siseko arrives home, it is before 6pm, the time his father has stipulated for him to return. His clothes are still damp. He changes immediately into a T-shirt and tracksuit pants and puts the wet clothes into the basket for Lusanda. She smiles. She knows her brother well.

Mausi and the Big Bucks

One afternoon, Siseko is walking home from school with Nkululeko back towards Elias. They decide to go via the towers to see if there are any tour buses. It's more than ten years since Madiba won the Nobel Peace Prize and tourist opportunities have sprung up all over Soweto. Americans and Europeans want to go to the famous Vilakazi Street and to the Hector Pieterson Museum. Lately, there are tour groups stopping at the cooling towers for a bungy-jumping experience. Sometimes, if you can talk to the tourists for a while – especially the older ones – and if you can tell them about growing up in the township and do so with a smile and without any show of expectation, then they might give you some money. He thinks how pleased his father will be if he can stop on the way home at Sollie's spaza and buy a box of candles.

There are no tour groups around today, so they walk to the edge of the dam. The traffic still rushes past on the Old Potchefstroom Road in the distance. But closer to them the weavers in the reeds shout and chatter to each other while the males build their nests. Then a minibus comes bumping down the road towards them.

'Hey, Nkulu, come and help me untie some boats.'

It's the coach, Ryno, shouting out the window while the bus engine still runs. Nkululeko just sits there. He loves the paddling but it's a schlep to fetch the boats.

'Who's your friend?'

'It's Siseko.'

Siseko smiles a bit and lifts his hand.

'Why don't you join us?'

Siseko thinks of the time in the storm when they left the boats out and how cross Nkululeko said Ryno had been. Nkululeko smiles at him conspiratorially.

'If I can? Please,' says Siseko.

'Don't waste time. Jump in.'

As they close the door behind them, Ryno steers the minibus back up over the eroded dirt track towards the house where the racks are kept.

'Where do you live?' he asks the young boy.

'That side.' Siseko points towards the informal settlement. 'Elias.'

'Sharp. If you do well today, you can come any time.'

When Siseko and Nkululeko get on the water and start to paddle the guppy boats, it is different from the times before. Now the coach is right there. This time, it's actually allowed. And he's so keen to impress. Ryno's interested in their progress.

'Come, guys. I want four laps round the buoys. Then I want to see each of you do a fall-out and swim to the bank. They're doing flat-water proficiency tests at Wemmer next week.'

The two kids take off. Nkululeko's paddles rotate too fast for his speed, which, at this stage, is somewhat mediocre, despite the fact that he is much more competent than Siseko. Siseko pulls nervously on the blades – the boat feels wobbly at first but soon settles into a rhythm.

The water is quiet and the wind rustles the bulrushes. Siseko feels far from the world of homework and candles. The roar of traffic down the Old Potch Road is distant. The rhythmic splash, splash of their paddle blades becomes their world for a time. He realises that there is something special about this time: when you are on the water, you can get away from people who do not paddle; you are away from the other concerns of the world. When they have done their four laps, with Nkululeko waiting for Siseko, they come towards the bank.

'There's a race at Germiston tomorrow,' Ryno tells them. 'I'm taking the bus if you guys want to come. Free food afterwards.'

That sounds good to Siseko and Nkululeko – free food, a change of scenery and a whole bunch of fun in the boats. So they readily agree to be there.

Early the next morning, Siseko meets Nkululeko and the others outside Mike's house at Power Park. It's Saturday. There's a newspaper man at the entrance, hitting his gloved hands together as he breathes out frost-breath. Otherwise, the streets are quiet. By 6am, when Ryno arrives with the bus, there must be about eighteen of them waiting and they pile into the fourteen-seater. Despite the cold, two of the bigger guys are only wearing vests. Their muscles flex as they throw their bags into the back.

'Hey, Snake,' shouts one of the youngsters, 'how was the trip?'

'Ja, great.'

Snake is cool. Not too fazed by anything. He reaches into his front jeans pocket and pulls out a pair of shades. Siseko is impressed by these guys, intrigued. They somehow give off an air of confidence, of accomplishment. But they're not gangsters like the other guys from the township who've made it out there. Not at all.

'I heard you guys won medals!'

'Ja, we had some good races. But there were some fast guys there. You wouldn't believe it.'

Siseko wonders where 'there' is.

'Snake and Mausi have just been to the Africa Champs,' Nkululeko helps him out, 'in Tunisia.'

'How far is that?'

'It's far. You have to fly.'

'Wow.'

This is something. These guys are from Soweto, from Power Park, and they've been up in an aeroplane. Siseko is desperate to ask what it was like but he doesn't know these guys yet so he sits quietly, listening to Snake and Mausi talk nonchalantly about their trip: how Mr Ramaphosa met them to wish them luck; how they sat in airports; how they stayed in a hotel. It all sounds like a different world. But the thing he is most impressed by is the idea of these guys testing themselves against the best paddlers on the continent. Not only that, Mausi talks about going to the

World Championships next. Later, Siseko will find out how difficult it is even to make the South African team, but right now he knows so little that it is easy to dream big.

Later, they arrive at Wemmer Pan. A lot of cars pull up with boats on the roof and there is a lot of rushing around. Ryno seems to be calm, despite the chaos of life jackets, splash covers and race entries.

'Don't worry,' he says to Siseko, 'I'll sort things out for you.'

Siseko and Nkululeko stand on the paved terrace next to the water, watching the main race start. A man with a megaphone keeps giving them instructions but they seem to pay little attention. Then he calls:

'Paddles up ... Go!'

And they take off, leaving a seething mass of water behind them. The collective power driven from their paddle blades into the water is impressive.

Siseko and Nkululeko climb into the smaller, more stable guppies. Their race is three much smaller laps around orange buoys. At the start, Siseko is left behind a little but he soon catches up. Besides, it seems that most of the youngsters are just there to have fun. It's great just to have a change in scenery and a bit of an outing, but Siseko keeps thinking about Mausi and Snake and their stories of travelling and competing out there in the big world.

After the race, they sit on the bank, joking and laughing and, best of all, eating the free boerewors rolls. When the main race finishes, Mausi and Snake come in third in a double. At the prize-giving, they receive an envelope with money for their efforts. On the bus on the way home, Snake tears it open and, to the envy of the rest of the kids, passes Mausi a R100 note. Mausi sees Siseko eyeing it.

'This is small change, boy. The canoeing is fun but it can only take you so far. The club is helping me to study. I want to be a CA. That's big bucks.'

Sitting there, as Ryno steers the bus past Vodaworld and Hollard, Siseko has no doubt that Mausi, with his confidence, muscles and poise, will get there. Over the weeks that follow, Siseko keeps returning to the Orlando Dam in the afternoons.

Township Fun

Township life can be fairly dull at times, but Siseko soon finds that there is fun to be had in all sorts of places. Sometimes, on cold nights, the older boys from Elias Motsoaledi decide to organise a 'social event'. They round up the younger kids in the afternoon – and although some of them daren't refuse to take part, others are happy to have the diversion. Very few make excuses that they have to help their mother cook or their father with some menial job. In any case, they know that there will be consequences later for not agreeing to take part. Although the township is big, the settlement is small: everybody knows everybody. The kids are rounded up like goats and herded across the township to the dump, where there are many discarded tyres. A great race starts between some of the kids who grab tyres and start rolling them back up the hill towards the southern edge of Elias. Every kid takes a tyre – some of them roll two at once.

By half past five, it is starting to get dark. Some of the tyres are thrown onto a big heap in the middle of a sandy clearing and others are scattered haphazardly around them. Siseko and some of the others sit on their tyres chatting – too old to be pushed around but not quite the instigators either. One of the older boys, Shadrack, with the spiky dreaded hair, carries a 5-litre petrol canister to the centre. Some of the smaller kids start to cheer. The older ones feign disinterest. Shadrack pours the petrol into the middle of a tyre and a few more are placed leaning up against it. Then he stands back, lights a match and throws it into the centre. With a loud whoosh, flames leap into the air and the faces of the surrounding children are orange-lit in the glow. Gradually, the light fades as the petrol is burned, but the warmth continues to emanate from the centre as the rubber tyres burn. Shadrack, his brother Meshack and another of the older soon-to-be gangster boys, Lungi, are circling the crowd, looking for volunteers.

'Guys, who wants to be boss?'

Shadrack grabs Siyabonga by the arm. 'Siyabonga is the champion!'

Siyabonga knows what this is about. He will have to wrestle for the entertainment of the older guys and the crowd. He is flattered by the recognition as Shadrack lifts his arm into the air, but he also knows that there is no truth in the claim at all – he has hardly ever fought and certainly not here at one of these bonfires. Shadrack becomes the fight promoter, jumping around, drumming up support and hysteria.

'Who's the boss of Elias? Who can beat Siyabonga?'

Siyabonga smiles nervously as he anticipates the challenger to come. Then, in an unfortunate twist to the plot, Shadrack turns to face Siseko and Ratabele.

'Ratabele will do it!'

Ratabele is horrified. He knows that he can almost definitely beat Siyabonga in a fight – he's nearly two years older – but he has no desire, let alone reason, to fight his good friend.

'Choose someone else,' he shouts back. 'Siyabonga is my friend!'

'That's unfair,' says Siseko – but not too loudly as he fears he'll only make himself a target.

'He's scared!' shouts Shadrack. 'Look at this guy! *Woyinkenkw'intwe encinci!*'

'Not at all!' Ratabele protests. 'That's not true!' The good-natured smile is gone from his face.

'He says he'll fight,' shouts Shadrack, and immediately the two friends know there is no turning back.

Within moments, they are shoved towards each other and become a bundle of scuffling arms and legs. Ratabele is caught off-guard as he trips over a stray tyre behind him, and he falls backwards on to the ground.

Dust flies and the mob shouts, crowding around them. But he's angry now and he soon overpowers Siyabonga. He climbs on top of him and forces his good friend backwards into the sand. Siyabonga doesn't resist – there's no real loss of honour in being beaten by an older boy and at least he'll be left free for the rest of the night.

'We have a winner!' shouts Shadrack in ecstatic fervour. He pulls Ratabele up and lifts his arm. 'The boss of Elias.'

Siseko can see where this is going. Once Shadrack is excited, there's no turning him back. Siseko takes out his trump card – an old, half-full Doom can – from inside the tyre he rolled and shouts:

'Doom can!' The kids who have experience in tyre fires cheer.

'Throw! Throw!'

He walks forwards towards the middle of the fire and lifts a warm tyre with his shoe.

'Watch out! Here it comes! Now!'

He tosses the can into the tyre and rolls it into the centre of the burning mass. The ring of kids widens as they scuffle backwards – at the same time, each trying to seem less scared than the next. White eyes blink nervously from the dark. It's suddenly quiet.

'Yooooh!' someone shouts, then laughs with bravado.

Another few seconds pass.

BAH!

The can explodes with the heat of the fire – township fireworks. Shouting and cheering kids jump forward again. A smaller kid pats Siseko on the back.

'Nice one!'

For a while, there's great excitement and the younger kids talk excitedly. The flames die down again but the warmth of the burning tyres still permeates the air. Slowly, the older kids form smaller groups, chatting quietly with their mates. There are very few girls there, but the few who are there command some attention for a while.

On the far side from where Siseko's group is still chatting, one boy, Sandile, takes another aerosol can from his jacket pocket. He's been debating with his friends for the last half-hour about whether to use it.

'Do it!'

'I'm not sure.'

'Come … we're going now.'

'I'm not sure I should.'

'You're just scared!'

'I'm not scared.'

'You are. Come, we're going now!'

The young boy takes the can, puts it into a tyre and rolls it towards the centre. It bumps into the first surrounding tyre and falls flat. In disgust, he rushes forward to pick up the tyre and pushes it with all the force he can muster. It ramps over the middle of the bonfire and lands on the other side – where Siseko and his crowd are about to leave. They're busy picking up a few last pieces of rubbish and throwing them into the fire. A large box lands on top of the tyre and they watch the flames flare up around it. The flames light their faces orange as the three stand watching. Men like to watch a fire they've lit burn – boys even more so. For the second time that night, there's a massive explosion. Remnants of the cardboard box are blown into the night. The three kids jump backwards in fright. Siseko lifts his hands to his face just as the lighted cardboard hits him. He turns and runs automatically into the dark. Then the pain is searing, excruciating, and he screams.

The other boys run to him. 'Quiet, quiet, you mustn't tell.'

'*Ngifuna inyama yam!*' he shouts. 'I want my flesh!'

'We'll get in trouble!'

'*Ngifuna inyama yam!*'

'Let me see,' says Ratabele.

Siseko's right cheek and hand have been singed. The skin is dark red and already welts are forming.

'I think it's not so bad,' Ratabele says. They have no idea that damage is being done all the time.

'*Ngifuna inyama yam!*'

And Siseko starts to run off into the dark. The night air stings his face as he runs – leaving the fire and the others but not the pain behind him.

His mother takes one look at her son's face and knows that he must go to the hospital as soon as possible. She wraps a wet rag around his hand

and tells him to hold it to his face while she rushes next door to ask Auntie for help. Siseko's father is working a night shift.

When he and his mother walk together, along the dirt path and up to the gates of Baragwanath, Siseko is still in extreme pain. But he takes pride in not showing this or complaining. If there's one thing Siseko has learned about himself, it's that he's as tough as they come. His wounds are dressed and, in the early hours of the morning, he is sent home. The nurse tells his mother that he must lie in bed and rest for a week.

The burns will be painful but the boredom will be worse.

Nkosi Mzolo

Nkosi Mzolo wakes early for his first day at his new job. For the time being, he and Loveday Zondi are sharing the garage outside Jacques' house. He notices that his nose is freezing. During the night, the highveld cold has crept under the garage door and across the cement floor. An early autumn cold. He smiles. It is not unlike the early morning cold in the valley. He dresses and, as he is pulling the bowls and spoons out from the cardboard box that serves for now as the kitchen cupboard, he hears Loveday getting up on the other side of the curtain.

'Morning, brother,' he says.

'Sharp.'

He is pleased by the thought: two young men born a stone's throw apart in the Umgeni valley – a few kilometres from where the Umgeni River eventually joins the Msunduzi River – and now living here, in Johannesburg, determined to make a different life for themselves. It has already been a rocky road for Nkosi, less so for Loveday. Perhaps today will be the start of better things for him, he thinks.

Nkosi came to Johannesburg in the hope of finding work – a career, even. His first job checking tyres at the transport company didn't work out so well. He was blamed for a puncture on a bus, which hadn't been put through his books, and when another investigation started around a second bus, which had come in too late, he saw the writing on the wall and resigned.

Since then, he has spent his days paddling twice a day, training to win prize money at the weekend races and working twice a week in Jacques' garden to pay the rent. He met Brad at the dam, who gave him a chance, but then, just as he was getting his licence, there was the accident at Langlaagte. The driver of a Pikitup truck that was blocking his view of the oncoming traffic had waved him through – or, at least, that's what Nkosi thought. He edged forward and collided with a car, writing off the bakkie he'd borrowed from his new employer, Adreach. It was hardly his fault and Big Fish had been more than understanding, but still – it was time to put things right.

Later that day, he stands opposite Rosebank Mall, outside the offices of Adreach in Rosebank. An Indian woman hands him a small pile of documents in large paper envelopes. Some are brown, some white, with addresses printed on neat little labels.

'Oh, and here's your map,' she says, almost as an afterthought.

'Thank you, Ma'am,' he replies, trying to conceal his dismay.

'Will you be all right?'

'Sure.' His answer is not convincing. Not at all.

'Are you good with maps?'

'I'm not sure. I haven't really used one before.'

'Oh.'

'But it's going to be fine?' He's asking more than telling her.

'Okay, so … let's have the first envelope.'

He passes it to her.

'So it's number eight, Archimedes Street, Sandton. Have you been to Sandton yet?'

'Yes, Ma'am, once.'

It's true: Elna had driven them through Sandton once but he had no idea which way it would be from where he is now.

'Well let me explain how the map book works …' the woman says.

At half-past one that afternoon, Nkosi arrives at 8 Archimedes Street and hands over the parcel at the reception. He returns to the small white bakkie and looks at the pile of envelopes on the passenger seat. It has taken him more than half the day to deliver the first parcel. He's had to keep stopping on side streets to re-check the map and the names of the roads where he had to turn. Also, it was tricky when you had to cross three pages to get to the delivery address. And then the lady from Adreach – his new boss, he presumed – had phoned twice to ask him how he was going and each time he'd had to stop the car and put the hazard lights on to answer.

Shortly after 5pm, Nkosi returns to the Adreach offices, having delivered only two of the envelopes successfully. It's not a particularly auspicious start, but later he will go from strength to strength. As he parks the bakkie, he sees a fire engine head out from the Rosebank Fire Station across the road – lights flashing and siren blaring. The driver looks confident and calm in his seat, despite the obvious emergency of the situation. Nkosi watches him admiringly – such courage. It is quite a contrast to his own blundering day delivering mundane packages. This is a moment he will think back on for many years to come.

As the weeks go by, Nkosi becomes more and more familiar with Johannesburg. Before very long, he is confident and efficient. Whenever Brad sees him, though, he always asks the same questions.

'How's it going, Nkosi?'

'Good thanks, *Meneer*.'

Nkosi calls Brad '*Meneer*' – which somehow straddles the line between respect for his employer and the friendly banter of fellow canoeists perfectly.

'Have you started studying yet?'

'Not yet.'

'But are you looking around? Have you got ideas yet?'

'Well, I'm not sure.'

'What are you interested in?'

Eventually, Nkosi decides what he wants to do. He just needs to work out the right approach. One afternoon, as Brad sees him coming up the driveway, Nkosi greets him, crosses Baker Street and walks in to the Rosebank Fire Station. There he learns that he will need to start with a first-aid course. Once he has completed that, he embarks on a basic ambulance assistance course. He volunteers to assist in an ambulance and comes to an agreement with Adreach that they will give him leave to pursue this dream.

And so Nkosi embarks on one of the most taxing periods of his life. He works twice a week in Jacques' garden to earn money to pay his rent, he trains extra hard on the other three days to try to lift his level of paddling and he tries to win prize money in the Under-21 category on the weekends. The Soweto Canoe and Recreation Club (SCARC) pays him a small salary to train the younger club members, although he soon finds this role extends to driving around, organising and parenting these kids. This is something he will do for many years to come. At nights, he volunteers in the ambulance. He hurtles through the night, helping, saving and consoling. By the time that period is completed, he is physically drained, but mentally and emotionally stimulated. He knows he has chosen the right career path.

Soon he finds himself working a full week at Adreach and volunteering at the fire station three or four nights a week. Throughout this regime, he keeps coaching and training the SCARC kids a few times a week. Nkosi's life becomes a blur of catching taxis, working, coaching and volunteering. He is always at the canoe races driving the SCARC bus, but there is barely time for his own training.

One night, he gets a phone call from Brad.

'Nkosi. Where are you?'

'I'm at home.'

'I need you,' says Brad. The tone in his voice is unusual to Nkosi's ear. Is it nervousness? Fear? 'I need you to come with me to Soweto. Something's happened at the dam.'

Dark Times

At Orlando Dam in the evenings, the water mirrors the setting sun – gold and silver slivers are broken into fragments by the rhythm of the paddles and boats, and then re-form. Ryno stands watching his charges, proud and hopeful for their futures. It feels good to be here. There must be more than 30 kids on the water this evening. The familiar splash of a paddler falling into the water draws his attention. A grinning Luzuko swims, pushing his boat towards the bank. The most extraordinary thing, Ryno thinks, is how comfortable these kids have now become in the water. That alone seems a victory.

As the sun drops closer towards the horizon, two young kids paddle an old fibreglass K2. They look to their left – to where an empty boat floats aimlessly on the water. Is it the white one that Luzuko had been paddling?

'Luzuko?' calls out the front paddler.

It's not like Luzuko not to put his equipment away.

'Come, let's finish up and if it's still there, we can put it away.'

'We should move the boat now. What if it sinks?'

'Ah, it's not sinking. It's going nowhere on this dam.'

'Okay, sharp.'

The sun twinkles behind the bulrushes, the last rays catching the leaves, rustling in the wind. Then the wind drops slightly and the sun is gone.

'Ryno!'

Ryno's attention is drawn from the bump and scrape of the kids climbing out of the water to a small boy running towards him.

'Ryno! We can't find Luzuko!'

The panic in his voice is clear.

'Okay, relax, guys. Where did you last see him?'

'We saw his boat, floating there. You know the white one?'

'Where'd you see it?'

'There it is.'

In the dusk, the white boat is just discernible, floating on the water. Ryno feels a slight flutter in his stomach.

'Hey … guys,' he tries to supress the panic, 'has anyone seen Luzuko? Did anyone see him walk up? Did anyone go back up to the house, to the racks?'

Ryno starts to run towards the bank nearest the boat – the other paddlers following behind him. The reeds on the bank opposite rustle in the night breeze, the water laps at the water's edge, but there is nothing much else to see.

'Okay, Sifiso, Magetsu, run to the container and check there. Then come back quickly.'

He's wading into murky water.

'Who saw Luzuko last? Did anyone see him paddling?'

'Sure, he was paddling.'

'Then he fell out.'

'Ja, we saw him fall out.'

'But then he was swimming.'

'Ja, he was swimming. Swimming this way.'

'And he was fine.'

'Did he look like he was swimming fine?'

A glimmer of hope.

'He can swim … but not so good.'

'Nah, he can swim good. He's better than you!'

'Okay, so he was swimming. Was he pushing the boat or just swimming to the bank?'

Ryno is almost waist-deep in the water now, shouting.

'No, he was pushing the boat in front. Like you showed us.'

'So he was swimming this way. Then did anyone see him get to the bank?'

The silence tears at the confusion.

'Phineas, Duma, run around the far side. Maybe he's behind the reeds there. And stay together … Everyone else go back to the container. Put your kit on and wait there. I'm going to look around a bit more.'

Ryno wades aimlessly in circles in the water, as deep as he can, his feet squashing through the thick mud at the bottom of the dam.

Jacques' phone rings at 8pm.

'Ja, ja, Big Fish. Okay. Shit. Ja, I'm coming. Yes, okay, my car … I'll be waiting.'

The first warning is the blue flashing lights as they park the white bakkie near the shacks at Elias Motsoaledi twenty minutes later. As he opens his door, the wailing of women shocks Brad to the bone. It is a startling, frightening sound. Ryno approaches his car.

'Jacques, he's gone.'

Ryno looks downcast.

Jacques is speechless.

Turning pale, Brad shakes his head. 'What can we do now?'

'The police are here. They want to talk to us.'

Moments later, the three of them stand facing the sergeant's confused eyes.

'So you started this swimming thing here on the dam?'

'We started the canoeing club some years ago, yes.' Brad takes the lead.

'This boy, this Luzuko, he was swimming here with your club tonight?'

'Yes, officer, he was paddling here and then he fell out of his boat.'

'So he was here, on the dam, swimming in that boat? Then he fell in the water?'

'That's right.'

'And then he couldn't swim?'

'Well, all the guys have to do swimming lessons at the pool here. And then, when they can swim, they can start to learn to paddle.'

'But this Luzuko, he couldn't swim?'

'Yes, he could swim. Luzuko had lessons at the pool here at Power Park. He could swim.'

'But where's he now then? If he could swim, he must have swum to the side?'

'I'm not sure. The kids say they saw him swimming towards the bank.'

'But they say he drowned? How can you drown if you can swim?'

Ryno steps forward. 'Officer, I was here, standing on the bank.'

'And then what happened?'

'The guys saw him swimming towards the bank. And then … he must have got into trouble.'

A voice from the crowd: 'But why you bring these things? These boats? These white man's things?'

'We were trying to build something …'

'Building what? Where's this Luzuko now? You say he can swim, but where's he now? What are you going to tell his family?'

Voices wail. A crowd seems to be gathering around them.

'Look, Officer, we can't answer that question. What we can say is …'

'This is too much talk. The boy's gone. What must his family do without a boy?'

'Officer, please, do you need to take statements?'

'First you must answer our questions,' a voice interjects. 'Have you been to the family?'

'Not yet.'

'You must go to see the family.'

'We must talk to the family, yes.'

'First you must come to the police station to make a statement. Then you can come back to see the family.'

'Well, okay …'

A frustrated murmur: 'Ah, you won't come back!'

Brad suspects this might be true. At that moment, he's a white man in the middle of an informal settlement. He feels far from safe.

Against the Grain

Ryno sits behind the large wooden desk, staring at Brad. He hasn't slept properly in nearly two weeks.

'Just give it some time,' Brad says, his voice lacking all its usual energy. 'These things need time. Have you been to see anyone, talked to anyone?'

The traffic stirs outside. The suggestion is ludicrous. They both know it.

'It's not going to make any difference, Fish.'

'You can't ignore the good that's being done by this club.'

'There was also a drowning, and you can't ignore that.'

'I know it's tough for you.'

'The whole time it's me at the dam. It's me with the community. And now this …' Ryno pauses. 'They don't even want me around there any more.'

'But hang in there. You've done so much for the club. Things will change.' As he says this, Brad wonders if it's true.

'No, look. I've done my bit.'

'You've done more than your bit. And that's why we need you to carry on. The club needs you, the kids need you.'

Brad's words are imploring, but his tone is far from it.

'Okay, Mr Fisher, I'll give it some thought.'

It sounds to Brad as if Ryno would like to give some thought to anything but this.

'Please do. And I'll always be here to back you up. Let me know if you need anything.'

'Okay. Thanks. I'll see you on the water.'

'Definitely. I'll see you later in the week.'

Ryno closes the door behind him, leaving Brad alone in his office. Brad stares at the empty desk in front of him. He knows that Ryno has borne the brunt of the disaster. Ryno's a buoyant character. He's forever joking and laughing on the water. But there are no smiles now, none at all. He's felt the full weight of responsibility for the death of a young boy. Ryno has needed his support, and he wonders whether he could have done more.

Later that day, Brad's shifting issues around his desk, unable to focus, when his phone rings. It's someone from the Gauteng Canoe Union office. First the usual pleasantries, but soon he's leaning back in his plush leather chair answering the same questions Ryno has been asking himself.

'Yes, he'd done the flat-water proficiency … Yes, Yes … They all have to go through the swimming programme.'

The questions continue for a while. Then they become more pointed.

'No,' he responds, 'no, he wasn't wearing a life jacket. They are supposed to, but they don't always.'

The voice on the other end is incredulous. Almost accusatory, he thinks. Or is he just being overly defensive?

'Well, there weren't always enough. And eventually some of the guys started paddling without them. Yes, I was aware that sometimes the guys got on the water without them … No, I'm sure you didn't know that. Of course you weren't aware. But I suppose you never paddled there, so how could you?' His blood's boiling underneath this statement, but he lets the point go. 'Yes, I'm sure you're busy. We're all busy.'

The conversation continues like this for a while, Brad's mood worsening. Anger suppression has never been a strong point and he feels stretched.

'What do you mean, "Were we affiliated to the provincial and national bodies?" SCARC was begun as a GCU development initiative … I can also just throw my hands up and walk away.'

For the next few minutes, Brad loses interest in the conversation. He says what needs to be said so as not to create unnecessary unhappiness.

When he eventually puts the phone down, he's annoyed, but he knows what he must do next.

Brad sits facing the man he so admires. His business associate of many years now, Cyril Ramaphosa had been the patron of the Soweto Canoe and Recreation Club almost from its inception. But one of Brad's greatest assets is his ability to talk to everyone with the same regard. He's appropriately respectful but never intimidated. The business issues are dispatched with efficiency and in a positive manner. This is a good thing because Brad's feeling exhausted. Yeats expresses it in the only way that does it justice, 'his soul stretched tight across the sky'. Now there's an elephant in the room and he knows he has to put the issue to bed.

'Cyril,' he starts, 'you read my email?' It's not really a question. Just a way of starting the conversation.

'Sure, I read it. I have to say it really disturbed me, my friend.'

'Look, I really think it has to be left alone now.'

'This initiative is close to my heart though, Brad. I think you might be responding too harshly to this situation.'

'Sure, but a kid's dead, Cyril. And the club is responsible.'

'Yes, but the club's also responsible for getting a whole lot of other kids off the street.'

'True.'

'And without you, this club would've folded several times.'

'It would have died a natural death. Maybe we should've let it go.'

'All worthwhile initiatives need encouragement.'

'I just think that there are easier ways. Ways that maybe make more sense.'

Brad's speaking matter-of-factly. He's put so much into this club but, right now, he just can't see a way forward. Cyril looks at him. Waits. He knows Brad loves this club. He knows how he must be feeling to have been brought to this decision.

'I've been thinking, what about if we keep the initiative going but we focus more on the other sports? The guys love the boxing. Half the population loves soccer.'

'Sure, but soccer isn't for everyone.'

'But there's not the danger of the water.'

It hurts him to say it, but at that moment he feels it's for the best.

'You'll lose your enthusiasm for this thing. I know you and I know how much you love this sport.'

'I'll put together a proposal. I'll commit. I believe in what the club is doing.'

'Don't forget that in a few short years you've taught hundreds of kids to swim through this programme. If you keep going, that could be thousands in the future.'

'I suppose,' he looks up, not enamoured with where this statement is headed. 'But I'm not really prepared to take that responsibility any more. I've seen how it's affected Ryno. We've lost him. And I know how it's affected me over the past few weeks. If we're going to run this thing properly, we need someone to really take the reins and I just don't have the time at the moment. I can't do it half-heartedly and feel that I'm not endangering these kids' lives.'

'Let me ask you something,' Cyril pauses and looks at his friend. 'You said in your email that this kid wasn't wearing a life jacket.'

'That's true, he wasn't.' He's hardly in the mood to be defending this point again.

'You've given reasons for that and I understand why not. But if he had been, would he have drowned?'

'It's highly unlikely.'

'So can't we work on increasing the safety aspect and push on?'

'But someone needs to be there every day at training times.'

'I'm going to tell you something. And I want you to listen. Then I think you should go away and give this some more thought.'

'I'm listening.' Normally, he wouldn't be listening at all at this point. But his regard for the man in front of him is immense.

'You know, when I was a boy … for a time, we lived in the suburb opposite that dam. We weren't allowed near that dam.'

'Really?'

'It's true. And you know why?'

'I've heard that Power Park was for white government employees who worked at that power station. The black guys weren't allowed anywhere near there. Is that true?'

'Yes, that's also true. We wouldn't have gone near that suburb. But we would've gone to the other side. Near the dam wall. We played on the koppie on the other side, but our parents told us not to go anywhere near the water. If I'd been caught there, my father would've given me such a hiding.'

'Really?'

'Of course. None of us could swim. We were taught to fear the water because it's dangerous. Even today, most of our population can't swim.'

'No, look, I realise that.'

'But do you realise the life skill you're giving these kids? Do you realise that, to this day, I can't swim?'

That takes Brad by surprise.

'It's true. I can't swim. And if you allow this club to die now, you'll be denying a lot of people an invaluable life skill.'

Brad sits still. He meets Cyril's eyes. He nods. His old friend is pleased to see there's a determined look on his face again.

After that, a posse visits eleven schools in all. Of the eleven, eight of them shun the SCARC initiative outright. But three are interested. Three of them see the value in a club that can be brought to the community. It's true that some of the kids don't come back, but many of them do. Through an enormous effort, the club begins to grow again.

Fire Fighting and Travelling

The basic fire-fighting course is three months long. Nkosi saves money for a year and then approaches Adreach. He negotiates three months' leave. The first month will be paid and then he'll be on his own. It also proves a challenge getting on to the course. There are only twelve places available. One warm, late summer's evening, he arrives early at the Brixton Fire Station in the hope of bagging a spot on the course. The trial is simple – a 2.4-kilometre run and they take the first twelve. That's it.

'One run? Is that the full trial?' he asks the friendliest looking of the three firemen there.

'That's it. Up to the robot, turn left. The first twelve back are on the course. No excuses, no questions.'

During the next 30 minutes, the numbers start to gather. By 5pm there must be close to a hundred guys hanging around. And three girls. Nkosi shakes his head at the obscure criterion. But he's fit and strong. He really wants this.

A short fire-engine siren squawk sends them off. A mass of backs and legs bolt up the road at a ridiculous pace.

Soccer players, thinks Nkosi. They'll get tired.

He keeps calm and runs hard. They head up the hill with the cemetery to their left. The early sprinters start to labour as the hill drags. As they turn at the top, Nkosi has time to count each runner in the dusky light. Fewer than twenty are in front of him. After ten minutes, he's dragged himself to the front. He's alongside the leader. Ahead, he sees a fire engine and he puts in a sprint and the breathing behind him regresses quickly. 'Left, left!' shouts the fireman as he approaches. He's pointing past Nkosi – behind him. Realising his mistake, he turns and races back to the turn he has missed. Four contenders have passed, but Nkosi sees red. He digs deep, passes them and gives it 100% round the last 300-metre loop to the finish. He's first in: on the list – done and dusted. They take his name and number with a promise to phone him.

The weeks drag and Nkosi starts to worry. He phones and gets shifted from pillar to post. Eventually, he gets told, 'Don't worry, you're on the list. We'll call you.'

The SA school's sprint championships take place at Nagle Dam in KwaZulu-Natal. Nkosi drives a busload of kids from Johannesburg to the dam, which forms part of the Umgeni river system. It lies just a couple of kilometres above his place of birth. It's a long trip though – with sixteen kids excited about the three-day tour away. For many of them, it's their first time away from home. Shortly after passing Harrismith, he gets the call for which he's been waiting.

'Nkosi?'

'Yes?' The usual pleasantries follow.

'So the course starts on Monday, 8am.'

'Monday?'

'Yes. It's at the Lenasia Training Centre.'

'But I've been phoning and you're only notifying me now?'

'There were problems with booking the centre. But it's no problem. I can put one of the others in. There's a long list.'

'No, I'll be there.'

'Okay. We need the deposit of R4 000 by the end of the week.'

'But it's Friday afternoon already.' Nkosi looks at his watch. 1.32pm. The banks close at 3.45pm and he's nowhere. With a bus full of kids.

'You can just send me the proof of payment. I'll send you the details – the centre address, the bank details and my fax number.'

'Okay, but I'm away until Sunday. Can I pay on Monday at the course?'

'My boss says if you haven't paid, don't bother to show up.'

'Sure? Ai ...'

'Make a plan.'

'Okay. Please send me the details.'

Nkosi drives on. The kids yell, but his mind's in silence. He's ecstatic. Incredulous too, though. He's got the money saved, but how on earth is he supposed to get it done in time? And the proof of payment. Then the trip back. The sprint races will finish at 5pm on Sunday. Then the course kicks off at 8am on Monday. He's obviously not in for much sleep. It's the best possible news he could have hoped for – at the most inconvenient time.

Two hours later, Nkosi parks the bus outside Standard Bank in Langalibalele Street, Pietermaritzburg.

'Guys, I need your help,' he appeals to the busload of kids. 'I need twenty minutes. Please, don't go anywhere. I'll be back as soon as I can.'

'You can't just leave us. Where are you going?'

It's Thapelo. His first trip.

'I'll be right here. I just need to go to the bank. And the post office.'

Nkosi disappears into the red-brick building, his forehead beading with sweat. But he's timed it just right. The teller is only too keen to get the transaction done to get out of there on Friday afternoon. Ten minutes later, he rushes out of the door, shouts 'One more!' at the bus and races down the road to the enormous post-office building with his deposit slip in hand. He finds a similar situation there. Although he has to queue for fifteen minutes, when he gets to the front, his fax is done in no time at all. He exits the old imposing Edwardian building, heading back towards where the bus is parked – windows open, doors thrown wide in the stifling Pietermaritzburg heat. But they're all still there. It's a victory. He has never felt so proud of himself.

A horseshoe of steep hills covered in natural vegetation encircles Nagle Dam. The sprint course here must be one of the most spectacular in the country, possibly the world. Sheltered from the wind, the water surface is usually smooth. For most of the kids from Soweto, this is a new world.

By late Sunday afternoon, the events have drawn to a close. Siseko is there. He's just fourteen years old. To him, the weekend has been one of beauty, surprise and also learning. The Valley of a Thousand Hills, as he has heard it called, amazes him. The landscape seems to go on and on. The speed of the boys from the valley in their boats has caught him by surprise. Back in Johannesburg, it is simple. The fast guys are older. The youngsters like himself are still improving – but a long way off. The valley boys are skinny – lightweights like him. But they're also fast. He speaks to Nkosi about it and also to the KZN boys. He realises that they train harder. They're always on the water and they're training hard. When they do sprints, they put their heads down. They're determined. He begins to think that there could be something more than just fun in the sport.

They sit there in a group on the sand bank watching the prize-giving. An old white *madala*, John Oliver, with a long beard, hangs the medals over the winners' heads. When it's all over, they pack up slowly, the kids dragging their feet, tying the boats on to the trailer racks and finally getting back into the bus – despite Nkosi's hurrying them along.

Finally, at 7pm, they join the N3 to Johannesburg. It's a long haul home. Many of the kids just sleep. Nkosi has much to think about. The SCARC boys have done well. A few of them have won medals, filling him with pride. One of the boys, Sifiso, will hang his medal on the wall of his grandmother's shack – the only decoration in the hut – and it will stay there for some years.

The basic fire-fighter's training begins the next morning. He feels only excitement at the thought. He drives the bus on through the night. It doesn't cross his mind that he's never driven at night before until he reflects back a few days later.

Eventually, they drop the trailer at Power Park, where some of the kids climb out, and then Nkosi does a lap of the informal settlements – dropping off each kid outside his shack. Some of the parents come out to greet them and smile proudly as stories are told. By the time he's dropped off the last of them, it's after midnight and Nkosi heads back up Chris Hani Road to the highway. For once, in the early hours of a Monday morning, the highway past the city is nearly deserted. Still, he feels only excitement at what is to come the following day.

He gets home and sleeps for four hours but then he has to get up early because the bus is not for his own personal use. He takes a taxi into town and then another out to Lenasia. Eventually, at 7.45am, he is there and ready for the training course. It has been a whirlwind last three days – but he's there on time, ready to begin.

'Kade Ucabangani?'
'What Were You Thinking?'

Thursday nights are great. The bus goes to Emmarentia, to Dabulamanzi, for the time trial. The paddling is ferocious – ten laps of 1 kilometre each and three turns on each lap. There's always excitement and stories to be told in the club afterwards. 'War stories,' he's heard the *umlungus* call them. And the food is fantastic.

One night, Nkosi has given Siseko a lift to the dam in Brad's car. Nkosi gives him the keys to go and change at the car. He changes quickly and then has an idea. He needs to get his sprint boat from the house to the dam so that he can paddle it on Saturday morning. If he goes quickly, he can be back in twenty minutes and nobody will even notice. Brad said he'll be socialising for an hour at least. Nkosi has been teaching him to drive on the weekends so he reckons he can manage. He'll be able to get his licence in three months in any case. It's dark and cold so most of the paddlers have gone inside. He climbs into the driver's seat and starts the Vito. The Mercedes engine jumps to life – a lot more lively than the SCARC bus in which he's been practising. He pulls off and manages a three-point turn in the street without any trouble. He pulls off towards Greenside and it feels easy. Then a car coming the other way flashes its lights at him. And the next does the same. He realises his mistake and flicks the lights on. All the way to the house, he is nervous. When he gets there, there's no one there and he loads his boat on to the roof rack. On his way back to the dam, he starts to feel quite pleased with himself. It would have been such a long walk with his boat from the house to the dam. Sorted. He stops at the red traffic light on Barry Hertzog. Nearly done. Green. He tries to pull off but the car stalls. Keeping calm, he turns the key in the ignition and tries again. But the car starts to roll backwards and he steps on the brake. He looks in the mirror and is horrified to see a police car stopped behind him. He restarts the car and, in his panic, stalls again. The blue lights flash behind him. He turns the key and the car starts, but he can't seem to pull off. In moments, his world has fallen apart and there's a policeman at the window.

'What's the problem?'

'I think it's the battery.'

The battery is the first car part he can think of.

The officer is unusually quiet. 'What's such a *piccanin* doing with such a big car?'

'It's my boss's car.'

The policeman leans in and turns the ignition. The car roars to life.

'There's nothing wrong with this battery.'

'I don't know engines. But I couldn't start it.'

'Can I see your licence, please?'

Siseko feels nauseous. He reaches into the central console, feels around for Nkosi's licence and passes it to the policeman, who barely glances at it.

'This is not you.'

'Sure it is.'

Then the officer really looks.

'It's not even close. Please step out of the car.'

A while later, Siseko sits in the office of the Parkview police station, listening to one side of a conversation between a Sergeant Magoba and Nkosi.

'Do you know a Mr Ntondini?'

He's given the policeman Nkosi's phone number and Siseko sits staring at the floor. Gone is the smile, the confidence. This could be proper trouble. Sergeant Magoba grunts at the phone. Constable Tsia just sits there, looking at him.

'But can anyone pay the bail?' the sergeant asks. He grunts again. 'He's young. I don't want to put him in a cell.' After a few more grunts, he grabs a piece of paper. 'Yes, ja ... eight, nine, six, six.' He writes the phone number on a piece of paper and puts the phone down.

'Do you know a Mr Fisher?' he asks Siseko.

Brad's phone rings at the canoe club moments later, just as Nkosi comes walking towards him.

'Mr Fisher, this is Sergeant Magoba from the Parkview police station.'

This doesn't sound like good news. The noise from the bar at the club is fairly loud and hardly the ideal background for speaking to the police.

'Yes, how can I help you?'

'Do you know a Mr Ntondini?'

'Hold on a moment, please.' He moves outside into the cold. 'Sorry, just say again?'

'Mr Ntondini. Do you know him?'

'Yes, I do. Is there a problem?'

'I've got Mr Ntondini here at the police station. He's being charged with theft of a vehicle and fraud.'

Brad's mood changes. He puts his unfinished Hansa down on a table.

'He says you said he could take your car.'

This is news to Brad.

'Should I come there now, Officer?'

'How will you get here, sir?'

It's a fair point. 'Sorry, Officer, just tell me what's happened, please?'

After a short explanation, Brad ends the call and looks at Nkosi.

'Big Fish, these guys are causing trouble again. Sorry.'

'Can you give me a lift there, Nkosi?'

'Yes, of course. But what are you going to do?'

'Well, the first thing I need is my car.'

'True. But I ...' Nkosi hesitates. 'I don't think you should just pay the bail.'

'Well, let's go and see.'

They arrive at the police station and come to an agreement with Sergeant Magoba. Siseko will spend the night at the police station but they will let him sleep on the floor in the office rather than in a cell.

As he lies on the floor, Siseko is distraught. He feels like he has let the side down. Badly. He's uncomfortable and disappointed. That night, he hardly sleeps.

Early on Friday morning, Brad and Nkosi arrive at the police station. Brad pays the bail and, a little while later, Siseko sits in the passenger seat of the car, his head hanging.

'Where were you going?' asks Brad.

'I wanted to bring my boat to the dam. I needed it for the weekend. I thought it would just be quick and I wouldn't have to bother anyone.'

'Why didn't you just walk with it like normal?' Nkosi asks.

'I should have walked.'

'Why didn't you?'

'It takes long. But I should have walked this afternoon.'

Nkosi just shakes his head.

Brad smiles to himself. Hazy memories from his time spent at the University of Cape Town, more than twenty years earlier, flicker at the edge of his consciousness. At that age, he was far more of a reprobate than Siseko has ever been.

'*Kad' ucabangani?*' asks Nkosi – what were you thinking?

When they eventually drop him at the SCARC digs, he gets quietly out of the car.

'Sorry for the trouble, guys.'

'See you on the water,' Brad smiles at him.

Road Trip into the Valley

The fourteen-seater bus is packed full as it pulls on to the highway in the early morning darkness. Orange neon lights race past overhead. The kids in the front seats talk excitedly of the days ahead – who will get to Durban first and who will wrap their boat on the way.

'Hey, watch out for Hippo. Remember what happened to you last time?' jeers Sipho.

'Ah, I won't make that mistake again!'

'Sure. Don't be like Big Fish – you must learn from your mistakes!'

The others laugh disproportionally to the joke. They laugh partly because their mentor and sponsor has broken his boat at Hippo Rapid three times, but more so because they are so excited to be heading out of Johannesburg on a five-day road trip. What could be better? For some, it's a break from the monotony of shacks, primus stoves and lukewarm washbasins.

True to the universal laws of bus etiquette, the older, more experienced boys sit at the back of the bus. The trip to KwaZulu-Natal means more to some of them than a few days' getaway from the monotony of their daily lives – it's an opportunity to put their training into practice. It's a chance to show that they're faster, stronger, tougher than the rest. But there's also something else. Some of them are starting to make it –

111

and it's through the canoeing club that it's happening. Andile is redoing Science for his Matric. Without SCARC, there'd have been no second chances. He's living in the SCARC digs and he's got a job to support himself while he's doing all of this. That puts him in a different league – he moves up the hierarchy. Siseko's achieving all of this but he makes the back row just by being the fastest paddler in any case. Sifiso's in the back row because he's a rebel. Tom's personality's his qualification. Mess with Tom, and he'll take you out with a serious put-down.

The bus crests the plateau and begins the descent down Van Reenen's Pass. An electric storm hangs threateningly over the Drakensberg to the west. Where such natural beauty exists, it's possible for one's dreams to seem easily achievable. As the land falls away beneath him, Siseko sits quietly, daring to allow thoughts of success and a gold medal in the great race to enter into his mind for the first time. There are so many tricks, so many nuances to the race, that he knows it will take not just a supreme effort but also more than a little luck to achieve that.

'Try to just sit and follow the guys where you can,' I had advised him.

'You've got every reason to succeed. Just put your head down and go,' Brad added.

In the rare silence of the after-lunch stop, Siseko marvels over the changes that have taken place in his life since he first traversed this mountain range fourteen years earlier.

Disappointment and Opportunity

Two thousand participants and at least another 2 000 'hangers-on' – seconds, friends, family members – settle into Pietermaritzburg for the three-day epic that is the Dusi Canoe Marathon. The people of the city themselves embrace the race as their own. The bustle of the pre-race registration is tangibly magnified in the midday heat. It can be oppressive, but in this group of athletes it takes on another nature. Some love it and soak it up with the hype and attention of the big race. Some find it daunting and try to slide away from the media attention. No participant wants to spend any more time than necessary in the heat of the sun, though.

Siseko has weighed his boat and he's heading for the coolness of the trees. He's pleased to be starting in the front row. He's quick off the mark and, if he plays his cards right, he could make the front bunch off the start and, from there, anything can happen. His thoughts are interrupted by a paddler he's never met before: Matt Bouman. Matt is six foot four, with the physique of Zeus.

'Just move to the side and I'll come through and pull you to the front,' smiles Matt.

A surf-ski paddler of unquestionable pedigree, he's been seeded in the second row for the start, and thinks he'll try his luck with the short, black guy occupying the front row directly in front of him. Siseko smiles back.

'Sure. See you tomorrow.'

Siseko's even more determined now. Off the start tomorrow, Matt Bouman won't even get to his wave.

The next morning, at only nineteen years old, Siseko grits his teeth and waits for the cannon to fire. As the rope lifts, he's off. By Ernie Pearce weir, he's lying fifth. All the way to the first portage, he sits with the front bunch, holding his own among the top paddlers in the country. When they get out to run for the first time, his body goes into oxygen deficit as he struggles up the path. He hasn't trained the change between running and paddling enough and soon the other guys open a gap on him. As the day goes on, he loses positions during the running sessions and makes up places on the paddling. But, towards the end, with the big portages, he loses more than he gains. On the last paddle in, from Cabbage Tree to the end of the day, he struggles to keep concentrating and finishes thirteenth – exhausted.

Over the next two days, the possibility of a top-ten finish slides elusively away from him. A massive effort on the last paddle in to Durban secures him a disappointing eleventh place – the first silver medal.

As he watches the prize-giving, he feels a sense of despondency. But as he thinks things through, he comes to the conclusion that it's just a lack of experience that has prevented him really excelling in this race. As the afternoon drags on, he becomes more determined to achieve a result in this race. Later, he overhears the winner of the race, Lance Kime, chatting to a mate. He plans on waiting until the last paddler comes in to congratulate them.

'I hear Piers has smashed his boat and is still trying to get to the finish. They sent the chopper up a while ago and they reckon he's not that far off now.'

Siseko hears this and sees an opportunity. He knows I must've noticed him coming up through the sport. He's pretty sure he stands out from the rest and that I would've seen that he doesn't give up easily.

Siseko sits on the bank, waiting for me, while the paddlers start going home and the officials start to pack up. Some time later, he sees a dejected paddler walking along the bank and goes to meet him.

PART 4

A New Partnership

Climbing into a K2 with someone for the first time is always a unique experience. Everyone has their own style, their own way of shifting their weight around, their own way of making the boat go fast. The first time Siseko and I paddle K2, it's a Thursday night-time trial, a ten-lap race around Emmarentia Dam. He's light. In fact, I hardly feel his weight in the boat. This is unusual for me – at 72-odd kilograms, I'm a lightweight myself as far as competitive paddlers go. But at that time Siseko weighs in at around 65 kilograms. It's a pleasure.

The most obvious way for us to sit in the boat is for me to drive and Siseko to follow. I have the experience of both rivers and race strategies. He is the faster paddler and the better all-round athlete. It's a combination that could benefit us both. When he shifts around in the boat, I barely notice. We paddle fairly well that night – and when we go to the front of the bunch, I can see the other boats are straining to hang on to our wave. Unfortunately, there aren't many competitive boats on the water that evening, but still – we feel pretty confident, and we have every reason to believe in our combination.

I pull up the driveway at around seven that night. When I open my door, my four-year-old daughter Emma comes running.

'Daddy!'

She jumps, catches me around the waist with her legs, and I hold her close. I know these moments won't last forever.

Later, once both she and our year-old son Dominic are asleep, Shelley and I sit at the table in the kitchen, chatting. Shelley's a great second, dedicated like you can't believe. She's been known to jump out of a moving car and leap into waist-deep, grubby Dusi water to make sure I get a replacement juice bottle in time. The race is exciting, fun. But it's the long hours training that take their toll.

This evening, she's been at home with a five-year-old girl and a one-year-old baby, cooking supper and getting them ready for bed while I've been 'playing' on the water. This is about the fourth time I've agreed to do my last really competitive race.

'How was it in the boat?'

'Ja, great. We dropped the guys.'

'That's awesome!'

'Hmmm,' I mumble. 'No one really fast was there.'

'Still.'

'Still,' I agree, 'it's a promising start.'

But I know the first real test will come in a major race – the Fish River Marathon.

All of the races have their own unique character. The Fish is raced between Grassridge Dam and the little town of Craddock in the Eastern Cape. A narrow belt of green trees and irrigated farmland splits the semi-desert scrub as the river winds its way through the Karoo. It's always a competitive race.

In the weeks building up to 'The Fish', I realise that Siseko and I aren't communicating all that well. But then I wonder if this is a matter of language, and perhaps culture. How much miscommunication happens because one person either thinks they understand when they don't really, or pretends they understand because it's easier than to keep asking questions?

At the start, we get off reasonably well and we're lying just inside the top ten as we snake through the willow trees that overhang the river in the first stretch of river. At 'Keith's Flyover' – the biggest rapid on Fish –

we swim and my paddle snaps. By the time we've got a spare paddle, we've lost a lot of time, but we're making up positions pretty consistently.

Towards the end of that first day, the boat starts to feel heavy, despite our relative speed. We're up to about 25th position and we've been leading our bunch for about fifteen minutes and I can see the other paddlers gritting their teeth, struggling to hold on to our wave. I drop my calf to the bottom of the boat, trying to feel if there is any unnecessary water in the boat. We've been communicating better over the past week, so I shout to Siseko:

'How's everything, you strong?'

'Fine, I'm fresh.'

'Good, and the pumps?'

'Sure we got pumps.'

'But are they working?'

'Ja, they're working.'

'One hundred per cent?'

'Hundred per cent!'

I glance backwards to my left to see a good stream of water shooting out of the left outlet. Then to the right, but there is barely a trickle of water coming out.

'Are you sure? The right one doesn't look so hot.'

'Nah. I'm fresh, not too hot.'

'Sure. But the right pump. It looks like it's not working so good.'

'Ja. The left one's good. The right one's not working so good.'

'Keep pumping and we'll be fine. But keep checking and don't forget to tell me if something's not working in the boat.'

Silence in the back of the boat. We put our heads down and paddle even harder.

We're not particularly happy with the result in the Fish – we know we are fairly on track, but we still feel frustratingly far from our potential, especially in the paddling. My natural stroke rate is far slower than Siseko's. And it's difficult for him to put in the same amount of effort as normal when he just wants to 'rev' faster. It's easier for a paddler with a slow stroke rate to follow a faster rate from behind.

But I'm reluctant to put him in front of the boat. It will add extra psychological pressure to him and will decrease the advantage of my years of experience in the sport. All the glory is in the front of the boat. The front paddler makes the decisions, chooses the line through the rapids, sets the pace and calls the race strategy. I love the front of the boat. Sitting in the back requires 100% commitment to the decisions made by the front paddler. In the back, you need to read the driver's mind and follow his every move at the moment – not after – he does it. It takes time to get used to and adapt to his style. For years, by then, I've been paddling with Jacques Theron. I'm used to his style – physically and mentally. I trust his decision-making. The idea of sitting behind Siseko is not an attractive one for me. He's young and talented, but not experienced.

•

'Hey, Steve, I see you've got some affirmative action happening in your boat? You'd better be careful. Before you know it, you'll be out of the boat altogether.'

Geoff smiles. Steve frowns, looking more than a little indignant in the back of the boat.

'Maybe you can come back as a consultant.'

•

There are a few chuckles from the audience – maybe some nervously recognising themselves in the role. The film has captured events like this, which might have happened. They're in the spirit of things at the dam. And, at the time, I feel a lot like Steve. Sitting behind Siseko in the boat is just not an option for me … And then there's portaging. The Dusi is the only major race in the world that requires so much running with the boat on your shoulder. It's uncomfortable and unpleasant. It's hard-core. And if you paddle at the back of the boat, it's faster to run at the back too. And running at the back, you can't see where you're going on the twisty paths and the weight is much heavier – it really sucks.

I have always loved running – aged 12, representing Pridwin School in 1987.

Winning the Grand Traverse World Sea Kayak Championships with Colin Simpkins in 1999. The helicopter almost blew us over.

Wearing my national blazer for the first time in 1999 – between great paddlers Graeme Bird (left) and Alan van Coller (right).

Winning the Fish River Marathon with Graeme Bird in 2000.

Big smiles at the finish of the 2001 Dusi – fifth place and a gold medal.

A life highlight – winning the Non-Stop Dusi with Thulani Mbanjwa in 2009.

Typical hospitality from the Mbanjwa family after the 2009 Non-Stop Dusi.

Shelley Cruickshanks has always been a great second – running here with Jacques Theron on Day 3 of the 2010 Dusi (© Sally Cruickshanks).

Training with Siseko Ntondini on the Melville Koppies (© Nick Warren).

Straightening the boat down Ernie Pearce weir shortly after the start of the 2014 Dusi.

The relief and ecstasy of the finish of the 2014 Dusi.

Brad Fisher (far left), Siseko (left) and Thando Ngamlana (right) after the 2014 Dusi.

Filming *Beyond the River* at Orlando Dam (© Robbie Thorpe).

The relief and ecstasy of the finish of the 2014 Dusi.

Brad Fisher (far left), Siseko (left) and Thando Ngamlana (right) after the 2014 Dusi.

With Brad (to my right) and Siseko (to my left) and the SCARC crew at the finish
of the 2014 Dusi.

With our biggest fan – Shelley.

Who would have guessed that our friendship would inspire a movie?

With the whole family on board!

Filming *Beyond the River* at Orlando Dam (© Robbie Thorpe).

Siseko – champion of the Lowveld Croc Canoe Marathon in 2015.

With the actors (and great guys) who would play our parts in *Beyond the River* – Lemogang Tsipa (right) and Grant Swanby (far right).

Musical Chairs

One Saturday in early November, Siseko and I are down on the water of Emmarentia Dam doing the 2 000-metre interval sessions. The routine is to get on the water at around 7am and the fastest paddler sets the guys off in roughly reverse order of ability. We all line up at the bank nearest the club and the slowest start first, followed by the next slowest, all the way through until the fastest guy leaves. We then complete two laps of the dam, which is 1 kilometre long, sticking close to the buoys, and then rest together before starting the whole process again. If the handicap were perfect, we'd all finish in a tight bunch together.

Siseko and I seem to be paddling better the more time we spend in the boat. We seem to get a fair rhythm going, but I'm not convinced it's good enough. I'm still looking for that 'feeling', a connection that's just not there yet. The sun is up and glinting off the water. It's going to be a beautiful day.

Brad is there paddling his K1. He gets off the water after six intervals while we carry on for another two. As we finish our last, he's standing on the bank with his phone.

'Hey, Piers, you must check this out.'

I'm not sure what he's on about, but I'm in no mood for a technique session. All I want to check out right now is a hot shower.

'Come and check this out,' he persists.

He steps on to the jetty, holding his phone towards me.

'What's that?'

'Look at your guys' technique.'

'Do you mind if I grab a shower first?'

'While you're on the water, I just want to show you guys this quickly.'

He can be extraordinarily insistent.

I push the rudder right. 'Let's take a look,' I say to Siseko.

As we get alongside the floating jetty, Brad squats down and holds his phone towards me. It's hard to see too much and then I remember I'm wearing shades. I pull them off so that they bob in front of my chest, dangling on the elastic around my neck. I squint at the screen of his phone. He plays a video.

'Check your guys' technique here,' he repeats.

I keep looking. I can see us paddling, but, to be quite honest, with the glare of the sun and the moving water, it's difficult to make too much out.

'Ja,' I say.

'You see what I mean?'

'Hmm.'

I nod, trying to sound impressed.

'He's rushing you and you're not getting the support in your stroke.'

That sounds about right to me.

Brad insists until we eventually agree to do a test. He gives Siseko instructions to slow his stroke rate down and to try to bring in more of a pause before he catches the water. We paddle 200 metres hard, picking the pace up until we're at our top speed. We do this twice. We can get the pace up to around 19.2 or 19.4 kilometres per hour – a fairly good speed for a K2 but nothing to write home about. I pull over to the jetty where Brad's still standing.

'Listen, we're pretty tired.'

'Okay, now let's swap around.'

Here we go. I'm not interested. I watch Siseko as he climbs into the front cockpit. His whole demeanour changes. He sits up straighter, his head lifts and his shoulders seem more relaxed. We pull off and do a short loop.

And immediately everything feels different. It's like sitting in the boat with a guy for the first time. As Siseko picks the pace up for our first run through, the stroke rate increases to the point where I'm pushed to the edge trying to keep up. But the boat feels better underneath me, it glides more easily. We reach full effort and I glance down at the Garmin in front of me: 20.8 kilometres per hour.

The decision is made. Siseko glows.

Later, Brad sends the videos to my phone. I sit on the couch at home, watching them. It's obvious that Siseko has to sit in front.

Dog on a Leash

Grant and Lemo run with a boat in front of the city skyline. I sit on a rock – watching. I was hoping they'd choose to film right at the top, where I'd stopped earlier to admire the view. But they tell me the view through the camera lens is different. And I buy the argument. One thing I've learned is that Craig Freimond, our director, knows his stuff. He always listens, but when he makes a decision, he's seldom wrong. From here the power lines cut an ugly line behind the actors and I smile at the symbolism – a thoughtful touch. I have to admit that the actors are doing pretty well. Lemo keeps his stride in time with Grant's – alternate feet hitting sand in sync as they lope along the pathway.

A dog trainer stands to one side of the path opposite her 'actor' dog. Just as they fall in line with her, she calls the dog, holding up a biscuit, and he races under Lemo's feet. He jumps wildly, dropping the boat in the process. Grant turns to face him – irritated. I laugh inwardly at the dialogue:

'What's the problem?'

'I thought he was going to bite me!'

'What? Did you see the size of that dog?'

'Aai, the small ones have sharp teeth!'

'Do me a favour,' Grant starts to smile.

'You white people give your dogs cute names like uFluffy, u ... But where I come from, we call them uHitler, uOscar – names of killers, man.'

They pick the boat up and carry on running. The effect is fairly comical and I hope it will work on screen. I imagine it will. Craig seems moderately pleased and sends them back for another take – this time with the camera zoomed in a little closer.

It's a strange experience, this. 'A film inspired by true events.' Yes, it is. I sit there on the rock, watching the filming, thinking back to the real experience on which this incident is based ...

•

It was early in our running partnership. We were struggling to find a good rhythm running with the boat – not to mention paddling. On most afternoons, walkers take their dogs to the Emmarentia gardens and that afternoon there were a few around, not too many.

I'm feeling frustrated as we head back towards the dam with the boat on our shoulder. I've been hoping the running will be our real Ace of Spades. I've been training my running for ages and I can see Siseko is fast. He leaves me behind on the Westcliff stairs sessions and his time trial times are quick. But somehow we aren't 'gelling' with the boat on our shoulders yet. We're loping down the slope towards the stream when I feel the boat pulling me backwards. I slow, annoyed, and then turn to see Siseko taking the boat from his shoulder and throwing it down between himself and an attentive-looking Staffordshire bull terrier. The dog leaps – playfully, I think – at him. I can see the whites of Siseko's eyes clearly. He looks genuinely scared.

'Hey, shoo!' I shout. '*Voetsek!*'

The dog looks briefly in my direction but carries on leaping at Siseko.

'It won't do anything,' I shout, really believing it won't. 'Just don't show it you're scared.'

A chubby, middle-aged man higher on the hill trundles towards us, whistling ineffectually for his dog. I am tired from the run – running with the boat is always tough, even at the best of times, and I'm annoyed and getting angry with the situation. The frustration of the run is probably clouding my judgement, but I don't care.

'Hey!' I shout aggressively. 'Put your dog on a leash!'

'He doesn't bite!'

The dog is growling now, but not really aggressively, I think. Clearly, though, he's scaring Siseko.

'I don't care. He's interfering with us.'

The man is closer by now. 'Everyone walks their dogs here!'

'So what, the by-laws say put your dog on a leash,' I insist.

I suspect my argument falls into that category of being right but ridiculous nevertheless. Then the dog lunges forward and nips Siseko on the ankle. He makes as if to throw something at the dog, and the owner shouts.

'Gatsby! Gatsby! Don't be scared!'

Then he turns to me. 'They always run, that's why he chases them.'

I'm incredulous at his use of 'them'. And bloody Gatsby has actually bitten Siseko now. I've been proven wrong and now I'm really losing it.

'Put your dog on a leash or I'm going to take your flipping head off!' I shout at him.

I throw my end of the boat down, squaring up to him. I know I'm being completely overboard, but I can't help it. All my frustration at the running, the condescending manner he has with Siseko, comes rushing out at the poor bald man with the dog. He looks absolutely shocked as he grabs the dog and secures the leash.

Siseko looks at me, amazed at my temper.

•

My attention turns back to the scene in front of me. There's the humour and the 'racist' dog. Sort of, anyway. Then there's the relationship between the main characters. That's pretty accurate. I've become good friends with Siseko, I think. I wonder whether the real experience will live up to what the film depicts.

Injury and Frustration

From that day on, our paddling improves dramatically. Not only that, it seems that we're already finding some rhythm running with the boat. It's as difficult as getting a K2 paddling combination to work. The runner at the back has to keep his stride in time with the runner at the front. It works best if the boat sits on opposite shoulders and the back runner plants his left foot in time with the front paddler's right foot. There are bio-mechanical reasons why this works best that one doesn't need to understand to know that it works. When the synchronisation happens, the boat flies with you. When it doesn't, the boat moves independently of the point at which it's perched and quietly goes about the business of removing the skin from your shoulder.

But on one beautiful early December afternoon, we're flying. We float through the dappled shade thrown by the tall trees at the top of the Botanical Gardens. At this moment, I have no doubt that in less than three short months Siseko and I will have achieved our goal. Sure, there's a long way to go and there will be challenges ahead, but it's easy to believe we'll get there.

There's a shuffling of the boat as we slow to turn around the 'big tree'. An enormous eucalyptus stands like a giant overlooking the lawns that stretch away beneath it – the grass that has flown beneath our feet so easily. Then there's a wrench on my shoulder as Siseko stops dead in mid-stride behind me, pulling me up short of the tree. Annoyed and frustrated at his lack of consideration, communication or whatever the issue is, I bite my tongue and lower the boat to the ground.

'What's up?' I ask, making what I think is a fine effort to hide my frustration.

'No, it's my leg.'

He really does look concerned. He bends forward and runs his fingers over the outside of his right calf.

'How sore is it?' I ask, all annoyance forgotten in my concern.

'I can run, but it's sore when I run.'

'When did it start?'

'It was sore the one time at the stairs.'

Memories, like short video clips, of our running sessions on the Westcliff stairs flit through my mind. The dark, icy sessions have been an integral part of our training for the past two months. I run the stairs throughout winter, maintaining my leg strength for the Dusi season.

'How long ago?' I wonder out loud.

'Just the last time.'

Last week, I think.

'Is it sore when you walk?'

'Only when I run.'

'And now? When did it start getting sore today?'

'When we started up the hill. After maybe 200 or 300 metres,' he says.

I can see he's deep in thought, carefully choosing his words. I'm not sure whether he's doing this because he wants to make sure he gives me the answer I want to hear or because English is not his first language.

'Why didn't you stop?' I ask the obvious question.

'You know how sometimes when you train hard,' he explains, 'your legs can be sore the next day. And then when you keep running, it becomes not so sore.'

I nod. 'Sure.' I know exactly what he means. As your muscles loosen up, you're freed of the stiffness. 'But does this feel like it's sore from training hard, or does it feel sore like someone has hit you with a pole?'

'Nobody has hit me,' he laughs.

I can't help laughing too. Although my stomach twists with nerves.

'No, I just mean what does it *feel* like. Does it feel like something has hit you there or does it feel like a sore, tired muscle?'

'It feels like as if something has hit my leg there.'

'I think we should jog slowly back and finish paddling our five laps we planned. If it's still sore in the morning, then we'll get you to a doctor.'

'No, Piers,' he seems vaguely incredulous. 'It's not a big thing. It's only a bit sore. I'm sure it's going to go away after a few days.'

'Let's see how it feels tomorrow. There's no harm in seeing a sports doctor just to make sure.'

We hoist the boat to our shoulders. I lead the way, jogging slowly back down the path, mindful of the fact that Siseko might just have described a stress fracture. At the same time, I'm desperately hoping this isn't the case and that he has somehow, unknowingly, bruised the side of his calf.

The next day when Siseko runs his leg is painful. And it's worse the following day. That evening, when I get home, Shelley can see I'm downcast, completely despondent.

The next afternoon, we approach the entrance to the Rosebank Sports Clinic. I find doctors' rooms depressing. They seem to me a good place to get sick: all these sick, lame people hanging around in a confined space waiting to have viruses or bacterial infections diagnosed and confirmed. Sports clinics are different, though. They're filled with sportsmen and -women recovering from injuries, rehabilitating their muscles to allow them to perform at their physical peak. I feel Siseko's spirits lift as he sees the gym equipment, the photographs of famous sportsmen crowding the walls and the youthful, healthy-looking clients waiting in the reception area.

Dr Jon Patricios approaches us with a smile.

'Thanks for seeing us on such short notice,' I begin.

'Let's hear about the problem, Siseko.'

A short while after we've laboured through the process of explaining how the injury has manifested, we stand looking at X-ray images of white fluorescent bones. The bones look smooth. Healthy. After Dr Patricios points this out, I allow myself to feel the first pangs of relief.

Moments later, Siseko lies back on the bed, resting on his elbows. Dr Patricios holds his ankle in his left hand.

'I'm going to have to press the area of the injury to try to gauge what's causing you this pain,' he explains.

Siseko nods.

Jon presses his thumb firmly into Siseko's skin and our world suddenly falls apart. Siseko rocks his head backwards on to the inclined bed and lifts his entire body off the mattress. As he does this, he begrudgingly lets a muted shout out of his mouth. He's clearly in extreme pain. And that's despite the fact that we can see he's doing his best to hide it. After a few more prods from the doctor and a few more levitations from Siseko – which would be humorous if it wasn't our dreams being torn apart – Jon starts his explanation.

'So sometimes you can't actually see these small fractures on the X-ray. It can be a crack so tiny that we don't see it, or it can be a stress injury that is about to crack and starts manifesting as pain for the patient before it's visually evident.'

'You're sure it's a stress fracture?' I ask.

I look at Siseko. He just looks terrified.

'It's certainly manifesting as such,' he continues. 'By the way you're reacting when I push on the fibula, it would appear that you've got an injury to there. Let's call it a stress injury, rather. The best-case scenario – and I think the most likely scenario, and this is the good news – is that we've caught the injury early. This means it will probably recover faster than most stress fractures.'

I nod.

'... But that still means that there should be no forceful weight in the area for at least six weeks.'

I make a quick calculation. The Dusi's in twelve weeks. That doesn't leave us much time.

'After that, would you expect him to start training gradually again?'

'I think so. That would be the expectation.'

Everything about this doctor seems measured and guarded, I think. I guess it comes with the profession. I look across at Siseko. He looks devastated.

'But there are some things we can do to assist the healing process.'

We both look at him. Expectant now.

'You can wear a boot air brace. That will enable you to walk around without exerting pressure on the leg.'

We both look at him, nodding. Then a thought crosses my mind.

'What about running in the pool?'

'That's definitely a good option,' he responds. He turns to Siseko. 'What you can do, Siseko, is put on your life jacket and float in the pool. Then you go through the motions of swimming while you float. So your body is supported but you can still work your muscles to a degree.'

'I can show you,' I add. 'I've done it before.'

'But there's also a new machine we've got here. It's an anti-gravity treadmill. Now I'm going to send you down to the biokineticist who'll fit a boot for you. Then I'll meet you at the gym and show you the treadmill.'

Later, Siseko stands awkwardly on the treadmill in the middle of the gym. Jon zips a black lycra suit up around his waist then presses a few buttons on the digital screen. The capsule surrounding Siseko's legs starts to expand as it fills with air. He stands there, bemused.

'Okay, so you can feel this thing pushing you up?'

'It feels good.' Siseko smiles for the first time in 48 hours.

'I'm going to start the treadmill moving. Just start to walk slowly as you feel it.'

Gradually the black surface under Siseko's bare feet starts to move.

'Now I'll increase the speed and you must start to jog,' Jon continues.

Then Siseko is jogging, with a smile on his face.

'Do you feel any pain at all?'

'I feel nothing,' he smiles.

'That's excellent news. You can control this machine with the buttons here, like I'm doing. Keep it set on 30% of your body weight for now and then in weeks to come you can increase that too,' he suggests.

A few minutes later, Siseko is running. His stride is leaping with the treadmill, running at 14 kilometres per hour. He's smiling all the time.

As we're leaving after a three-hour visit to the centre, it strikes me how much time and expertise have been given to us. Although we've received terrible news, not for the first time I'm aware of how moved and motivated people are by the story of the Soweto Canoe and Recreation Club. We leave with an envelope of X-rays, an air boot, advice on how to adapt Siseko's training, free use of the latest technology gym equipment and a shattered dream vaguely stuck back together.

A bill never comes from Dr Jon Patricios or the Sports Centre.

After that, we train differently. We paddle plenty of sessions – on the dam and on the rivers. In the mornings, I drive Siseko to the Morningside Sports Centre where Dr Patricios has given Siseko free reign to run himself into a stupor on the anti-gravity treadmill. I run on the road and pavements past a mix of recently established complexes and high-rise office blocks.

From the very first time, when I get back to the gym Siseko is running flat out. His gazelle-strides threaten to take him right out of that machine. And he's still grinning. Soon he's running at 16 kilometres per hour – as fast as the machine will allow – for an hour. And he's increased his weight to 50% – meaning that his legs are now carrying half his weight while he runs.

Then one morning we go back to the Westcliff stairs. I drop Siseko at Shelley's parents' house, with a life jacket strapped to him, and leave him bobbing up and down – 'running in the pool'. I run the stairs – ten times up and down the stairs – and by the last few sets, I can't go any faster. At the top, I reach down and lean on my knees for at least a minute, just trying to breathe. Then I put my hands on my hips and stare back down at the stone steps, which have taunted me all winter with their relentless incline. The view over the jacaranda-speckled northern suburbs is magnificent if you can look. Mostly, I can't. There can be few sessions harder. It's just less than 500 metres from the bottom to the top, but there's a height gain of nearly 100 metres. After the last one, I take a moment to savour the achievement and this time I do look out over the hills. A cuckoo calls from his hiding place somewhere in the canopy below. Then I take an easy trot back to see how Siseko is getting on. A suitably satisfied trudge down the driveway ends my session. Siseko's sitting on the grass. He's fully dressed and even has his towel wrapped around him.

'What's up?' I ask.

'Ja, it was cold,' he says through quivering lips. He looks freezing.

'And the running? Did it work?'

'It worked.'

Running in the pool is amazing training. Your leg muscles can work against the resistance of the water – replicating the running motion precisely without any impact on the skeletal system. I look at Siseko. His lips are a dark purple. As far as I know, that's the last time he tries running in an outside pool.

Return to Dangwani and the Mountain

It feels good to be back in the familiar green valleys and hills of the Eastern Cape. Nothing is ever as memory preserves it, of course, and with time comes change. Days playing in the river and the long grass fill Siseko's head and he smiles at the images of the days he loved. He knows though that this time will be different and although he has not played like that for many years, soon those times will be undeniably banished from his frame of reference. The great mystery of the mountain will soon be revealed to him and when he returns to the city in a few weeks' time, it will be as a man. Yes, he and some of the other guys are living in the SCARC digs – living away from their parents, they make their own decisions, look after themselves. But he's seen the other young men who've been through the ceremony. Sure, they're city boys now, but still they have a way of asserting themselves. It's in a knowing glance or a nod amongst themselves. Siseko's no traditional boy, but he will be proud to have been to the mountain.

The ochre dust lifts into the air as the bus pulls away. Siseko and his parents start to walk up the long hill towards his grandmother's mud-

and-stone house. Siseko kicks an old Black Label beer can into the grassy gutter. The mealie plants look tall and healthy and there must have been good early rains. The old house looks as it always has – homely and welcoming – and half of his being is filled with nostalgia for the second time that day. A part of him is critical, though. How long would it take to just fix the door hinge? And the roof is rusted. Maintenance is slow to happen here. A part of Siseko knows he can never live a rural life again. Before he can get to the house, his youngest cousin, Ntombizodidi, has spotted him and is shouting for the others.

'Siseko! Siseko! *Izapha!*'

Soon the other young children are running towards the three of them. They shout and greet from a great distance. As they surround Siseko, he can't help laughing and smiling with them. His father smiles too, knowing that his son will soon be a man. He is so glad that this time is now here. Some of the older children are less excitable but just as pleased to see that their cousin is back. Slowly and quietly, but with no less happiness, they leave the weeds and also start to walk towards the house. When his grandmother comes to the door, there is shouting and ululating. Ntombizodidi hugs Siseko's legs – it's as high as she can reach.

In the days that follow, Siseko joins the children in weeding and digging in the garden. It's fun to smile at him and the little ones look up to him. Soon enough, though, it's boring. But when his grandmother instructs him she does so differently now. She speaks with respectful eyes and a smile because she knows that it is only for a few more days that he must carry out such tasks. When the paraffin lamps are put out at night and the men are still talking outside, some of them still drinking beer, Siseko joins the children to sleep on the floor of the big room.

One night, there must be twenty of them all lying across the floor. He wonders how many times he has done this over the years – but it's been a while since the last time. He lies there in trepidation, knowing that these days are numbered. Soon it will not be acceptable for him to lie with children. And when he returns to Johannesburg and visits his parents, things will be different. He'll always be their son, but he'll never again be treated as a child.

A few days later, at dawn, Siseko's uncles and some of the elders, whom he has seen before but doesn't really know, come to fetch him. Quietly, without waking any of the children, the young boy leaves the house.

When Siseko returns several days later, there is great celebrating. Here the party is different from any in the city. Everyone is welcome. It is not just the little cousins who are excited and who shout. His grandmother is clapping and singing, the children are shouting and his uncles and aunts are beaming. His parents are proud of their son. A large, fat cow is chosen and slaughtered for the celebrations.

All of the family members are there. The ones who work have given money and clothes for Siseko. In fact, there is a completely new wardrobe waiting for him. There are two new pairs of shoes and a leather belt. Many of his old friends from childhood also attend. And more people from beyond Dangwani even arrive. There are men and women who greet Siseko with a broad smile whom he has never met before. He wonders if his father knows them. But these things are not important. What matters is that he has passed through the ritual. Tonight, and all nights after this, he will sit with the men. He's never been big on smoking, but he will drink beer and talk with the men. Not only that, he has noticed already that when he speaks, the men stop to listen to him. So he will need to think carefully before he starts to speak so he doesn't waste their time.

In the early hours of the next morning, when most of the guests have gone and there is just light on the horizon, his father calls him to talk with his uncles and the other older men. Siseko purposely lets the tobacco smoke infiltrate his clothes, even though he hates the smell. Tomorrow, he will smell of beer and smoke, but also of manhood.

Melville Koppies

I've been running these hills for weeks now. It feels like years. In sight of the old Jo'burg city skyline, the koppies rise like a relic from the past – and a last bastion of indigenous vegetation, yearning to be protected. Birdlife still flourishes here, almost as it always has.

'You even get moles there still,' Bulky once told me. And it's true. I've seen their little mounds popping up in places where the grass is short. They stop, though, if you go too near. As you run on the koppies, you pass the odd rusted tin can and glass shards twinkle threateningly just off the path, but it doesn't take much imagination to see how it once was.

It's mid-afternoon on a Friday. A wonderful time to be out running. My breathing is heavy but I'm feeling good. Siseko's away – 'at the mountain', somewhere in the Eastern Cape. But a good mate, Gavin Shuter, also training for the Dusi, has joined me for the session.

Gavin's about 30 metres behind and that only serves to motivate me more. Just before the path disappears over the hill, I turn to the left. There's a steep embankment and the rocks are big. It takes enormous effort to get up. I'm breathing heavily and my quads start to burn. Smaller steps help. I pump my arms, trying to keep the momentum going. It takes a heaving jump to the left and then one more to the right, and I emerge at the top. The view is a hazy, sun-glinting-off-buildings type of view. It's a pleasure every time. I love it. I hunch down over my knees and let my breathing come back slowly. Then I turn to look back down the steep and rocky path.

Where's Gav? Was my gap so big?

Then he bursts out from under the canopy, running well, running fast. Then he turns up the bank – the way I've just come – and his pace has to slow. It's steep. And tough. But this is why we come here. It's the best place in Jo'burg to train for the Dusi.

'Piers!' He's not even at the top and he's stopping to walk, stopping to shout. 'Piers, I just got held up.'

I'm catapulted from my euphoric chamber.

'There was a guy with a gun. He stopped me but I told him I had nothing.'

'What?'

'A guy just held me up.'

'Shit.'

'Just as I was coming round that bend under the trees.'

'That's terrible.'

'He said we should be careful because there are a lot of bad guys around here.'

'Ja, sure. Like him, maybe?'

'Ja, exactly.'

The afternoon breeze cools the sweat on my neck.

'Shall we get out of here? Shall we cruise?'

'Which way?'

'Let's go back the other way.'

'Okay. Shit, I can't believe this. This is our place. This is where I train for Dusi.'

'There isn't a better spot in Jo'burg,' Gav agrees.

'Fucking criminals, why should we not come here?'

Gav looks at me.

We're rock-hopping down the other side, quickly but carefully. Then we're on to the flat, following the path down. Not nervous, just disappointed.

A figure emerges on the path ahead. A grey-blue T-shirt.

'Hey, Gav,' I'm suddenly nervous of every innocent stranger, 'that's not him?'

'Where? Oh ... no, I don't think ...' We slow our pace, looking down the crooked stony path. 'No ... Yes!'

'Shit.' I'm off and skirting the path wide. He reaches behind his back and silver-grey glints in the sun. 'Shit.' I'm still running wide. 'Fuck.'

'Wait, Piers, wait, just do what he says.'

The man turns towards me, running now.

'We've got nothing,' I shout.

'Hey! Stop.'

'We've got nothing!' I'm veering further off the path and heading into the bush.

'Wait, Piers, just do what he says.'

'Ja, stop, Peerz, listen to me. I'll shoot you.'

Fuck it. I stop running. I stop thinking too. I'm just scared.

'We've got nothing. You can search us.'

'Just stop. I'll shoot you,' his voice is imploring but irritable.

'Okay, sorry, what do you want from us?'

'Don't look at me.'

I look at the ground. A rocky, grey, distorted ground. I know I need to be calm, but I can't control my racing mind.

'Come this way, don't look at me. Walk in front.'

'We've got nothing.' I'm starting to feel desperate now. 'Nothing on us. You can check. Just our keys ...'

'Don't talk.'

'Just do what he says, Piers.'

'Peerz, I'll shoot you. Just listen.'

'Okay, sorry, sir, we'll do whatever you want.'

'Just listen to me. Walk.'

I can feel the gun. Not physically, it's not against me, not at all. But it's there. At my back. It's the only thing I'm aware of. The only thing in my world as I walk down the rocky shelf. We're off the pathway and in a clearing. Surrounded by the shrubs, hidden from view. My stomach tightens, my world shrinks. It's just that glinting piece of metal. And fear. That's it.

'Keep facing away. And lie down.'

'Why? Listen, we've got nothing.'

'Do you want me to shoot you, Peerz?'

'No, sir. Do you want to take our keys?'

'Yes, we'll tell you where we parked,' helps Gav.

'Don't talk. Just lie down. Look at the ground, not at me.'

I'm lying on my front on the stony ground. The sharp rocks stick into my chest. Like acupuncture, I think. A strange thought. The dirt's in my nose so I turn my head to the left. Then it's just the gun I'm thinking about. And the back of my head. I close my eyes. Please … please, I think. There's shuffling to my right.

'Just keep quiet. You know there are lots of kinds of torture.'

'Please, sir, don't hurt us.'

'Just listen. There are lots of kinds of torture if you don't listen.'

'Sir, we'll do whatever you want.'

'Face the ground. And just listen to me. If you do what I say, you won't get hurt. If you don't, I'll torture you to death.'

The threat seems almost comical to me. Silly. But I'm not laughing. I'm just lying there with my face in the dirt and a stone pressing a divot into my chin. I'm just pleading, hoping, praying. The gate to my world opens slightly and Shelley slips in. Shelley and Emma and Dominic. I'm a father and a husband. And I don't want to die. I want to live.

I want to live.

'Sir …'

I'm back in the world.

Gav's voice is tight, almost desperate. 'Sir, why are you tying me up?'

'So you want to tell Peerz something, hey?'

'No, I'm just asking. We'll do what you say, but why are you tying me up?'

'Just stop talking and face the ground.'

There's more shuffling and it goes on and on. I wonder briefly how long this is taking.

'So tell me. Where did you park?'

'We parked at the Botanical Gardens,' I say.

'Where's that?'

'You know this road in front? It's Beyers Naudé. Left on this road and then first right at the parking lot on the corner. You know the one?'

'Why would you park so far?'

'That's where we park and then we run here.'

'Just face the ground. I'm calling my friend.'

He walks to the edge of the cliff and whistles. Then he's at my back and pulling my arms. He pulls them up, crosses them and starts tying them with something. It feels like some material cord. Then he's tugging at my shoes. All I can see is dust and stones but I imagine bright yellow trail shoes being pulled off my feet. Then he's tying my wrists again. Tighter. Too tight. Orange shoe laces cut into my skin around my wrists. I breathe the dust. Just don't kill me, I think. I've never wished for anything so much in my life as I do that afternoon. Lying with my face in the dirt, the world closing in around me, I wish, I pray, I hope for my life.

He whistles again. There's shouting in a language I don't understand, or even recognise. A foreigner – I think.

My ankles are pulled tightly together and now I'm helpless. Lying there in the dirt, just wanting my life. There is only one thought in my mind. And that is that I don't want to die. Death. A strange, black hole threatens me from the corner of my awareness and it's all I can do to push it away and stop it from engulfing me.

This is how people get executed, I think. Face down, shot in the back of the head. Didn't they find someone dead like that a few months ago? I push the thought away.

Then there are soft footsteps approaching and there are two of them in our world now.

'If you tell me where to find your things, I'll come back and untie you. If you don't, there are many kinds of torture.'

He sounds like a villain from a third-rate movie, I think. I wish briefly that there wasn't a man with a gun pointed at my head. Because then I could laugh. If there wasn't a chance that my head could explode and my life could end right here, then yes, I could laugh. But I can't. There is a man. And a gun. And now there's another man.

'Tell me. Where are your phones and your wallets? I'm going to take your keys to your cars.'

'My wallet is in the cubby of the car. And my phone too,' Gav answers quickly, urgently.

'And yours, Peerz?'

'In my car, next to where my left elbow is, when I drive, there's a compartment. If you open that, you'll find my phone and wallet.' I actually believe that if I tell him what he wants to know, there's more chance I might get my life back.

'Make sure. If you tell me right, we'll let you go. My friend is going to watch you until I come back. Are you sure?'

'Yes, please just don't hurt us.'

'Peerz, are you sure?'

'Yes, you'll find my wallet and phone there. Just please, sir, don't hurt us,' I say.

I suspect he knows I really mean, 'Don't kill us.'

Then we're lying there on the Melville koppies. We're far from the city, with the sun going down. We have no idea whether there's someone still watching us any more. The traffic hums in the distance, oblivious to our desperation.

'Hey, Gav,' I whisper, 'can you still see someone?'

'Hey? No. I don't think so.'

Silence on the koppie. Good.

'Shall we try and get out of here?'

'What do you want to do? Can you get up?'

'I don't think so. But we can try to leopard crawl.'

'Where to?'

'Anywhere. He's got no reason to come back.' Then I think to myself: 'Other than to shoot us.' But I don't want to say that, so I say, 'There's nothing worse than just waiting. Not knowing what's coming.'

'I'm not keen to try to do anything here. Maybe if we can leopard crawl to the bushes down there.'

Gav looks towards the edge of the cliff. I nod. I try to wriggle forward on my front but it's painful. The rocks are sharp and I know I won't get very far like that.

'Shall we try and stand up?'

'Okay.' Anything, I think. Anything but lying here waiting to be shot in the back of the head.

Gav shuffles, I squirm. I'm struck by how difficult this is. All the movies are nonsense, I think. My hands are tied too tightly. There's no chance I can get them out from under me. But Gav's up. He's up and standing. He can see over the rocks and around the koppie.

'Come on, Piers. Come on, get up!'

I try again. I get to my knees this time. But how the hell to get my feet underneath me?

'Come on. You've got to get up.'

I understand. But it seems impossible. I'm nearly up and then I fall to my right and I'm on the ground again. I try again. Then a third and fourth time. Desperately this time – and then, finally, my legs are under me, pushing me up.

'Okay, now where to?'

'That way.' He gestures to the cliff again. 'Let's get into the bush and then try and untie these ropes.'

'Okay.'

And I start to hop. Legs tight, arms behind us, and we're hopping. It's not easy. Again, I think, in another time, this might be funny. Ha, ha. Very funny. But right now, I'm terrified. I know nobody's coming back but I'm still terrified he might. The man. That man. The one I hate. The powerful one. The man with the gun.

We're hopping over rocks and we start to go down the cliff.

'I'm stuck.'

We're whispering, but I can hear he means it. I look back. He is too. Gav's shirt is caught on a bush. And there's a rock in front of him.

'Come on, Gav. You can do it. Just don't fall. But we've got to get out of here.'

He jumps into, through, over the bush. Somehow. It's impressive.

'Jeez, well done.'

We're under the cliff edge, into the bushes and out of sight from the top of the koppie.

'Okay, now what? Shall we try something here? If we just keep it quiet, no one will find us.'

'There's broken glass.'

'Try and pick it up.'

He reaches down, his hands behind his back, scratching in the dirt for broken pieces of beer bottle. He's got one. Then he's trying to turn it towards the ropes on his hand. It slips, falls to the ground. He tries again. Again, it falls. I can see it's futile.

'That's impossible. You can't do it if you can't even see your hands.'

'My hands are going numb. I can't even feel properly.'

'Let's try something else.'

I sidle up to the rock cliff. There's a sharp corner and I get my hands up against it. I try to scrape up and down on it. It rubs my hands too. I know it's useless. There's more chance of rubbing through my skin than through the laces.

'Maybe we should try to hop?'

It's a ridiculous thought, but what else? Two kangaroo-prisoners hopping in their socks down the Melville koppies at dusk to safety ...

'But which way?'

'That way. Towards the cemetery,' I say. 'It's open and safer.'

'Okay, let's just scan the path to check there's no one coming.'

We hop-creep further down the rocky bank, through the trees. We move as economically and quietly as we can, but actually clumsily.

We look down the path. It's the one where Gav was first held up. No one. We look up to the left. Westwards. The sun's gone down, but it's still light. The only sounds are the doves. And I think I hear a tchagra. It's hardly the time for that, I think.

'Now's as good a time as any.'

I look at Gav but he looks doubtful.

'Let's go.'

We start to hop. Over rocks, over grass tufts. We hop and bound.

There's still a shoe attached to the laces tied around my ankles. It swings round and hits me in the shin with every hop. Gav has a little friend too, kicking him in the shin with every hop. Then the laces start to feel looser. I stop, pull my feet against the laces, and they loosen. A little. Gav sees me, stops, does the same. A foot comes out! I pull and pull, it loosens some more. I stand on the shoe and pull with my other leg. My foot comes out. We start to run. We can run! We're getting away from the man and heading for safety. As I run, the shoe swings round still, hitting me in the shin. Sometimes it skips a step, somehow it misses. How considerate, I think. Then I feel the other side start to loosen. I stop and 'pull-push' with my feet and it comes off. I pick up Gav's shoe and we start to run again.

And that's us. Two athletes, running in terror, in their socks, through a graveyard. Running in fear, running in relief.

Training for Dusi 2014

In December, I'm on holiday with the family in the Eastern Cape. I use the time to train hard. It's light by 5am when I put my K1 on my shoulder and jog the roughly 1 kilometre along the beachfront to the lagoon. I turn away from the early sea mist and paddle up the Grootbrakrivier until a small low-level bridge, roughly 3 kilometres upstream. It's a pretty spot. One morning I startle a fish eagle fishing from his perch on a dead overhanging tree. Generally, I can get back to the house by the time the family is having breakfast between 7.30am and 8am. Shelley appreciates it – and sometimes looks at her watch good naturedly and smiles, shaking her head at me.

Later, I find the steepest dune on the beach and abandon the afternoon sand-castle-building efforts with Dominic and Emma to run a hill session up to the fynbos and back down to the point where my feet sink deeply into the sand at the water's edge. It's impossible to make my lungs burn like they do at Jo'burg's altitude, but I run until my quads feel like hard blocks, ready to explode. I run on the beach and paddle up the river again and again. I do sprint intervals, paddling, running with my K1 and then paddling again. Successful Dusi training is about training the individual components of the race but it's even more about putting those aspects together. After running 4 kilometres with a boat on your shoulder, you get back on the water and your arms feel weak and feeble. It feels like all the blood is in your legs and your arms are useless. The more you train the change-over, the better your body adapts.

Towards the end of the school holidays, I'm back in Jo'burg – feeling fit and strong. I'm quietly confident my form is good enough to compete for a top ten. Sure, Siseko's missed a lot of running training and I wonder how the mysterious rite of passage has gone. He's spent his own – I suspect rather different – two weeks in a different part of the Eastern Cape.

Owing to Siseko's injury, we've missed most of the qualification races so we'll probably be seeded in the second row. But I've got gold from there a few times before. Despite my concern over Siseko's form, I've a growing confidence in our partnership. We're becoming friends, building trust in each other.

The Sunday morning after we get back, I see Siseko at the club.

'So you're back from the mountain?'

'Ja, I'm back.'

'What should I say?'

'Sorry?'

'Is there a saying that you say? You know, like congratulations? Or well done? Or something? I mean, like when a guy comes back from the mountain.'

'No,' he shrugs. 'It's just like … then you a man.'

'Wow.'

'It's a big thing for us.'

'I'm sure.' It's quiet. I pull my vest on. I wonder what to say next. It's such a big thing. And I just haven't a clue about it. 'What was it like out there?'

'It's like you can't say what happens. You have to keep it a secret for the guys who are still to go.'

'Okay. Was it tough, though?'

'It's tough. You know, some guys …' he pauses, 'some guys, they don't survive.'

'Really? Even these days?'

'Ja, these days they make it much safer. Actually, I've never known someone to die.'

'But it still happens?'

'It still happens.'

'Wow. That's quite something.'

'It's a big thing for us.'

'Anyway, it's good to have you back.'

'Thanks, Piers,' he half smiles.

Before we know it, we're back into the full routine of training again. We're in the gym three mornings a week, running five or six times a week and paddling at least six times a week. When we take a rest day, it feels like an imposition. But from years of training, I know our bodies need it. We try to run off-road as much as possible to protect Siseko's leg injury from the impact of the road, but he has shown no signs of weakness. In any case, the more we run off-road, the better. There are only a few sections of tar-running on the Dusi and running on the uneven ground is important to practise. At nearly 40, I'm more cautious, less well-balanced and less flexible than my twenty-year-old partner. Another reason I would have liked to be in the front of the boat! At least I would have been able to see where I was going.

African Time

We're close to the race now. I'm starting to feel confident that we can actually do this thing. Even if we don't qualify in the front row, I have every confidence that we're fair contenders for gold. We've arranged to do a dress rehearsal at the time trial this evening. I'm fully kitted out in my life jacket, juice bottle – the 'full monty'. I've got the boat ready at the edge of the bank because it seems the SCARC bus is late. Or Siseko's late, in any case. But I'm not too worried; there's still fifteen minutes until we start. Standing there, facing the afternoon mid-summer sun, the light catches the water, forcing me to squint my eyes.

'What's this? African time?' an annoying mate jibes at me from on the water. I keep smiling. With Siseko in the front of the boat, we're fast and I know we'll be hurting that very same irritant in less than half an hour. I'm going to make sure we really make him scratch to stay on the bunch. But I just smile. Then Siseko strides past behind me, flicks a wave and keeps walking.

'Hey.'

'Hey.'

He looks a little nervous so I just smile at him.

After a few more minutes, I start to fidget. We needed a good warm-up to make sure we can really pump it off the start – practice for the race. Siseko's late and doesn't seem to be rushing. With five minutes to the start,

I pull the boat out and run towards the club. I search the change rooms. Tom, one of the established SCARC guys and Siseko's mate, is rushing out as I reach the door.

'Have you seen Siseko?'

'Ja, I saw him outside a while ago,' he frowns.

Strange. I rush back to the boat, but he's nowhere to be seen. The siren goes from the club balcony and the K1s take off. That's three minutes until we start. I turn and run under the bridge towards the racks. I grab my K1 and head back to the water just as the siren for the K2s goes.

'Sorry, Piers!' Siseko's behind me. We've missed the start.

'What happened?' I ask, the frustration and anger obvious in my voice.

'No, I still had to go to the digs, to fetch my kit,' he says, still apologetic.

It dawns on me. He'd got a lift to the dam and arrived in time – but slightly later then our planned early warm-up time. He'd raced across the lawn to where the SCARC bus was parked, jumped in and raced back to the digs to get his paddling kit. He must have really driven! But I'm furious now, seeing red.

'But why didn't you just tell me?' I shout. We're scrambling into the boat. He's got no splash cover with him. So much for the dress rehearsal.

'I thought I was going to be quick,' he responds quietly.

'Not flipping quick enough!' I shout – harshly, rudely. I'll regret my tone later.

We push off from the bank, chasing the tail-end of the field. We put our heads down and really pull. By the fourth lap, we've caught the front boats and I know we're in good shape. We'll be great, come Dusi. We go to the front, hurt them and eventually pull away by ourselves. But the worst is, I feel like a real idiot. I'm embarrassed at my unnecessary temper. I want to apologise so that we can enjoy the synchronous paddle – use it as a team-build for our partnership.

Afterwards, we stand in the warm breeze – the best time of day at this time of year.

'Hey, listen, I'm sorry. I shouldn't have shouted at you.'

'Nah, Piers, it's fine. I should have told you but I thought it was going to be quick.'

'I understand. Sorry, man – I was a real idiot.' I really do feel like an idiot.

'It's cool, man. Let's take the boat.'

'We paddled so well ...' I trail off.

If only that had been the focus of this conversation.

Dusi 2014

Day 1

Camps Drift. The big day. We line up at the start. The mist lingers still in the early morning sunlight. But we know the heat of the valley will engulf us soon enough. Three rows of twenty boats each. A hundred and twenty young men nervously point their boats east, towards Durban. We feel strong, so strong.

Helicopters hover above us. Loud – an unwanted interference. I focus on the line of boats in front of us, knowing we have to bridge the gap. We have to get as far forward in the field before Ernie Pearce weir as we possibly can. Then Siseko's right arm is up. I dig my left blade into the water behind his and wait … All I can hear is the 'tukka-tukka' of the chopper above. Water droplets fall from his blade, slicing through the mental stillness. A rope hangs – demarcating each of the first three lines.

The rope lifts. Power into the water.

It's a great start. To the left, boats are slightly behind us, to the right more so. Soon a diamond-shaped bunch forms in front of us and we're at the back of it. We're scratching around in the murky, swishing bathtub.

No clean water for us today. We approach Ernie Pearce – the pace picks up, then slackens. Twelfth. It's good enough. Great, even, given our second row start.

Ernie Pearce is so quick. You're at the top, then the bottom, just like that. I lift my paddle over the stopper wave as it engulfs Siseko at the bottom. The water roars and I dig my blade in, in sync. We're through cleanly and sprinting away, after the second bunch forming in front of us. Hank and Jasper are ahead, along with Andy and S'bonelo. Then it's Cam and Jakub on their own. Then there's a big bunch, eight or nine boats, but we're tucked in right behind them. And feeling ... great.

We wind left then right, stirring up the waters. Working hard, but comfortable. I can feel Siseko's frustration. He's fit, strong and young and he just wants to go. Then there's a chance and we're wide, out of the current and sprinting down the right. But Len moves wide, picks up the pace and we don't get past. Relax. It's a three-day race.

'Relax.'

The river tightens to the left. We're waiting for a gap, feeling good. Then the view opens in front of us and we're heading for Witness weir. The pace picks up again. Then the water's rushing all around us; we're heading down the weir, but there's mayhem. Thulani and Lance are out of their boat. Powder-blue deck and Kevlar across our line and we hit it. Siseko's paddle jams on the right, into the rocks. We lurch to the right. I catch it and roll up, but Siseko's out. Then I see it. His paddle's snapped and flapped back into place. My heart sinks.

Siseko's out of the boat and running up the bank. I jump out. Empty the boat. Push the tail down, twist, lift and empty. Boats are passing us. Push the tail down again, twist, lift and empty. So many boats. Then I'm back in and waiting. I swivel the nose round in the current. I'm facing downstream, waiting. The last boats of A batch are passing me, the cockpit in front of me still empty.

Still, I wait.

All the boats are gone. It's just me and the flowing river. The surprisingly loud roar of the rapid in my ears. I start to worry that the second batch is going to come through and add to our woes.

Then he's back. Holding my spare paddle, he climbs into the boat. We're off and charging down the river.

'It's only five minutes,' I say. 'Five minutes over three days. It's nothing. We can make it up.'

'Sure.'

I wonder very briefly if I'm lying, but only for a moment. Then the focus is back. Our paddles are digging in and we're pulling, twisting.

Through Mussons and the light is bright now. Sunlight glistens on the water. I hear Shelley's voice.

'57!'

But it's just a number. We're feeling strong and the boat is flying. We're through cleanly. Before the sewerage farm hop, we're catching a boat and we pass them at last, then another. One more before the portage. I look to my left and see Ric Whitton. With many Dusis under his belt, he looks at me and nods encouragement. He knows the pain of an early setback.

Out at the portage. Up the steps. It's muddy and slippery, the long grass pulled out of the ground in clumps. We're up, onto the flat and running. My breathing is fast but deep. Our legs stretch out and we're flying past a boat. And then another. Back in the water, we're still moving well. I try not to think too much about the boats ahead of us. I just focus on the paddler in front of me. I support every stroke, every movement.

'We're going well. Just keep going. We're catching.'

We're out at Pine Trees. It's a clean take-out and we're over the first bump. I look up and there are boats ahead of us. A long line of boats, glistening wet in the sun. To the right, the same. Some have taken out at the second option and a second line snakes up the grassy hill to join our path a few hundred metres ahead. So many boats. Now there's no denying the damage of our early setback. Or the challenge.

I feel the enormity of it pushing into my awareness. But I fight it back. I follow Siseko's footsteps. My breathing is loud and desperate now. We run. We run and run. We keep passing boats. We crest the hill. We haven't walked yet.

Then we're flying down towards the bridge, passing the mealie field to our left.

Then there's ice-cold water on my head. And Shelley is alongside me.

'31. Three and a half minutes to tenth.'

It's far better, but there's still a long way to go.

The acacia trees beckon in front of us. We pull off the path again and pass another boat. We're past them and racing down the hill, our boat behind us, dragging through the grass. We cross the rocky stream and we're slowed to a walk for the first time by the boats in front of us. Nkosi turns, sees us and moves to the side.

'Go, guys.'

We pass them and our momentum takes us into another boat. Two boats crash together and we push them off the path.

'Hey! Flip, man!'

'Sorry, sorry,' I just have time to say before we're in front of them and catching the next boat. The path is tight. Rocky. Uncomfortable to run on. Long grass tugs at our ankles. Thorns scratch calves – barely noticeably. Stones and rocks are uneven underfoot.

We're on to the dirt road. There's space to run freely. Properly. We pull wide and pass another boat. It burns. My lungs burn, my legs burn. But we're flying. Up and over the Hole in the Wall bump, Siseko's legs pump. I watch his calves glistening in the light. I suck for air. We're racing down the hill towards the river again. The boat's off my shoulder and we're slide-crashing down the bank.

In cleanly and into the flow. The boat feels comfortable. One with the current. We twist and wind – the boat feels great. Wisps of mist still hang, like old man's beard on the acacias, on the banks around us.

Guinea Fowl portage. Feared by many, revered by us today. We're out and moving cleanly. The paddles 'thunk, thunk' in the boat. The air's still but cool under the canopy. The light shafts through acacias. No time to admire, though. We're running. Still running well up the steepest part of the hill. And we keep passing boats. Every single one a prisoner taken back. A step, albeit a tiny one, towards our goal. Still, so many boats in front of us.

We're over the hill, rushing down the steep, grassy path and on to the jeep track. Our strides open and we're flying again. 'Thunk, thunk.'

'Coming through, please.'

Mark Mulder looks up. I'm surprised to see him. We're catching then; perhaps it's even possible? But I dispel the thought from my mind. Focus on the task. Dig a little deeper. But Mark shifts to the left, making space for us to pass.

'Thank you.' I waste energy, but it's worth it. What a gesture.

We're into the cauldron. Rank. Stifling. The cicadas screaming in our ears. But Siseko's on song. Flying through the dip, I'm pushing him up the other side. A few long strides – we have to walk. Big steps. Forcing the muscles to push us up the path. Our quads burn. The moment the gradient eases, Siseko's running again. I'm gasping for breath but I follow. We crest the hill and there's ice-cold water on my head again. And again. Never enough, it trickles down my back. Beautiful, but insufficient.

The boat's down and we're dragging it along Geoff's Road. Side by side, we're racing down the hill. The boat roars on the gravel behind us. I'm hanging in. I look across at Siseko – his face is grim. Determined.

Back in the river. And we're quickly into the current – it feels like our friend. Our rhythm comes quickly, easily. The water level feels lower, warmer. A few rocks graze the underside of our boat. 'Good,' I think. 'Slightly low.' It suits us. We're light and strong.

I can see three boats ahead of us. Maybe four. I'm thinking we might be back into the top twenty then. And I'm thinking, if we can just get to around fifteen today. Then maybe …

But before my mind drifts, I'm back on the task, following Siseko's rhythm. Then we're passing under the high bridge. Voices shout encouragement. Too many voices. The water splashes from Siseko's blades and I can't hear clearly. But Gav Shuter's at the bank.

'Fifteen, Piers, fifteen!'

It etches on my mind. 'Fifteen.' Three or four boats ahead of us, and we're catching. My mind struggles to comprehend. We're back in the mix. Our spirits lift.

'We're nearly there!'

'Ja, ten is right here. We're catching them!'

Through the next little rapid, we're on top of the bunch. One boat swims, fourteen. Then we're out of the current, over the wave and passing the next.

And the next.

Twelve.

We're up alongside the next boat, Shaun and Wayne. They push us wide, out of the current and we can't get past. Then through the next rapid, we're alongside again. And then … past them.

Eleven.

But we drift slightly left and they're in front again. Nothing asked, nothing given.

Twelve.

Finger Neck portage. We're taking out together. The air's hot, our breathing is forced. But we're past them before the top of the hill and racing down the other side.

Eleven.

Back into the water quickly, we're moving well. Tired, but loving it. Then we're racing up to the next boat. Loveday and Thando Ngamlana. Quickly up onto the wave. And then we're past them.

Ten.

The infamous Cabbage Tree portage beckons. The long tar road winds to the left up ahead. I can see Jacques and Shaun. Lucas and Mmeli just behind them – closing down on them. The tar road is steep but we're back in the mix. And our tails are up.

'Come on! This is nine, ten and eleven!' Bulky is spongeing ice-cold water on me. 'You're there! You're doing it!'

Our spirits lift again.

Up Cabbage Tree, Siseko runs. He just runs. No stopping, no walking, no resting. And I follow. We're emptying our tanks. Putting it all out there.

We're moving past Jacques and Shaun on the hill. Ice-cold water splashes on my head. The tar is wet, slippery underfoot. We don't stop.

Nine.

We're closing on Lucas and Mmeli. We're hauling them in. They're great runners. Solid paddlers. But the momentum is with us and we're chasing them down. Over the crest – it's a great relief. But then we're charging past them and down towards the dirt road. We're passing them. My lungs are heaving, but we're flying. We're alongside for a few moments but then past and heading for the water. The put-in is welcome, the river low and warm, but again we know it suits us lightweights. The last paddle is always hard, tough on the arms. The mind knows the job's nearly done for the day.

We come through the last drop feeling great. Thando and Loveday still on our heels, then Jacques and Shaun, then Mmeli and Lucas. All bunched up behind us. We cross the line.

Eight.

Our tanks are empty and I know it. But we're back in the mix. We're in the golds and up for a fight!

Day 2

I feel tired but strong as we warm up for the start of Day 2. An open, flat stretch of river with fairly fast-flowing water serves as a suitable ending for the first day and warm-up area for the start of the second day of the Dusi. We lean into the current as Siseko dips the nose of the boat into the moving water and spins us around to face downstream in good time for our start.

'Eight: Ntondini and Cruickshanks. And nine: Zondi and Ngamlana ... Ten seconds.'

John Oliver's voice, synonymous with canoeing, encourages us to the start line.

'Three, two, one, *go!*'

We pull off in unison, feeling the power against our blades propelling us forward. A few hundred metres after the start awaits a quick portage under Dusi Bridge. We pull to the right bank, standing and jumping out of our boat together, as we've practised so many times. But our move is a misjudgement of the conditions and exposes our lack of course knowledge as the boats of both Loveday and Thando and Jacques and Shaun pass us by, paddling closer to the take-out and jumping over the weir quicker than us. We push off the bank, frustrated by our mistake, and spend the next twenty minutes trying to find a way back to the front of the group. Our efforts are exacerbated by the fact that our bunch hauls in Damon Stamp and Mthobisi Cele. A big group of boats is not efficient in that stretch of river. Channels and small rapids keep forcing the boats to two abreast or even single file, meaning that aside from the boat in front, one has to keep dropping back and then pushing back over the wave. This wastes valuable energy.

The early morning mist has only lifted slightly as we drop through the last few rapids approaching the take-out point for the Saddles portage. The four boats fight for the dominant leading position and as we slide the nose of the boat up the slanted rock, the fourth boat catches our tail and spins our boat, forcing us to lose balance and time. With our boat quickly on our shoulders, we start running from the back of the group again. Just as we make our way to the front, Siseko rushes the river crossing and, in his haste to get quickly into the boat, jumps right over it and lands on the other side, chest-deep in the heaving, muddy Dusi. We quickly recover, once again relegated to the back of the group, and begin the run through the second saddle. Unfortunately, the last stretch of this portage is enclosed by thick vegetation and the slope of the bank towards the river makes overtaking virtually impossible. As we finally put the boat back into the water, we turn to see the eleventh-placed boat, Lucas Mthalane and Mmeli Cele, is close behind us. Once the threat of eleventh position is felt, the entire psychology of the bunch changes. Any position from fourth to tenth is an acceptable result to the competitive Dusi paddler, but eleventh is unmentionable.

The pace picks up as we approach the confluence of the Umgeni with the Umsindusi – on which we are paddling. We are briefly held up as Siseko drives us over the rocks in the approach to the first rapid. This leaves us struggling to maintain contact with Jacques and Shaun at the approach to the Ngumeni portage. Fortunately, we feel strong and run well over the tough Ngumeni hill. The gradient of the hill is steep and the boat weighs enormously on the shoulder of the runner at the back. The sandy pathway is eroded and we need to watch our footing as we work our way up the hill. My breathing is heavy and my chest heaves as we struggle up the winding path, ducking and pushing through the sparsely leaved acacias. Looking back at those points after the race, I'm always grateful for the months of training done in preparation for the race. But at the time, when the heart is racing at close to or over 200 beats per minute, the only thoughts are how to keep putting one foot in front of the other as quickly and efficiently as possible – and perhaps, briefly, a thought about the craziness of such a race.

Such doubts about the significance of our endeavours are fleeting, though, as we crest the hill and start to race down the dirt road, dragging the boats as we go. The relief from the exertion is replaced by the grind and roar of the boats dragging behind us on ropes. The risks are high: a lack of concentration could mean a fall and certain injury, running at speeds of close to 20 kilometres per hour down the gravel road. The river comes as a relief, with the knowledge that the rest of the day's racing will be on the water. We make one more mistake, getting stuck on the rocks in an innocuous rapid. The nose is caught in the eddy and we spin to the right and get stuck against the rocks. It takes an enormous effort to get back into the flow. Not a word is spoken though. There have been months of communicating, of miscommunicating, of trying to come to a better understanding between each other. Right now, there is no need for any of that. Our understanding of what is required from each other is perfect. The physical effort from our bodies is transferred into power on to the paddle blades in absolute unison and our boat surges through the current.

It has taken months of training, analysis of technique and strategy. But ultimately, 'feeling' the boat is a very difficult thing to describe. If you put your paddle in the water and take it out at the same time as the person in front, that's one thing – it's a good start. But different paddlers put more power in at different points in the stroke. As a back paddler, you have to try to sense where in the stroke the front guy is putting in most power and apply the same to your blade. When you get it right, the boat feels like one and there is a synergy created where it seems one plus one equals three. The boat runs smoothly and it feels like you can paddle forever. It's an awesome sensation. When you get it right, you just want to paddle harder and harder all day long. And forever. This is what I love.

We're in the zone for twenty minutes because that's how long it takes to catch the group in front. By the time we reach the flat water, signalling the approach to the magnificent Inanda Dam, we are paddling in a group of five boats, in positions seven to eleven. Simon van Gysen and Craig Turton appear not 200 metres in front of us on the flat stretches, and we know we will catch them. At Inanda Bridge, start of the infamous gruelling 9-kilometre stretch to the finish, we clamber for juice from our seconds and jockey for position. Incredibly and despite the mayhem, Shelley drops both of our juice bags in our laps and we are off across the dam. Jacques and Shaun pull a hard interval and lead us onto the flat waters. In the confusion, Lucas and Mmeli and Damon and Mthobisi are found wanting. We pull our paddles in momentary triumph and relief as we've established a group of four boats in positions six to nine across the dam. But any euphoria is tempered by the fact that this is a three-day race and we have to put time between ourselves and the strong running crews behind us who will have the advantage over the tough Burma Road portage on the final day.

Day 3

The sun is hot and hanging directly above us as we shuffle around awaiting the start of Day 3. The organisers shifted the start of the top contenders and to a reverse format, meaning that we will race through the heat of the midday. Siseko looks serious but not stressed when I see him.

'I'm thinking of wearing this cap,' he tells me, pointing to his yellow, Yum Yum peanut butter sponsored cap, 'to help with the heat.'

'Good idea,' I reply. 'The problem is it can trap the heat on the top of your head and make you feel hotter. Why don't we cut some pieces out for air vents?'

'Okay, sharp, Piers.'

We hack away at his cap until it is effectively a peak with supporting straps around his head. There's nothing like a simple task to take one's mind off the stress of the task ahead before a race.

We pull off for the start of the final day, four boats in a tight group, dwarfed by the surrounding mountains as we glide across the dam. The first portage is a tussle up a steep hill and then a crazy sprint down a gravel road to the treacherous Tops Needle rapid. We take the shorter, safer route and head for the channel that joins the rapid halfway down. We're racing, but the risk of shooting the whole rapid from the top seems imbalanced. We run into the knee-deep pool and push our boat off, putting our cockpit covers on as we glide. The cold, rushing water swings the nose of our boat left as we enter Tops Needle rapid, forcing us into the current. But Tops Needle has struck. Jacques and Shaun's heads bob in the rushing water; their boat emerges against the rocks, a broken, mangled mess of Kevlar and metal cable.

'Get your tenth!' shouts Shaun before we are out of the danger of the rapid and gone down the river. Simon and Craig have pushed ahead and have a slight lead on us and we chase them all the way to the Burma Road take-out. The rapids, Side Chute, Kindergarten and Umzinyathi give relief from the burning sun as the waves splash in our faces.

We take out for the Burma Road portage and are soon on Simon and Craig's tails. The clunking of paddles in our boats barely drowns out the screeching cicadas as we run. Showing true sportsmanship, they let us pass on the tight pathway and, before long, we have left them behind. Near the top of the hill, we are forced to walk for the first time in the race. The path is steep, surrounded by long grass and slippery – many feet have already passed this way earlier in the morning. Soon we crest the hill and the speakers blare loud music, sponges excrete ice-cold water on our faces and, in the hazy distance, we can see Durban. Siseko races down the hill, dragging the boat down eroded paths and over the long grass. As he reaches the flat dirt road at the bottom, I have to sprint to reach the tail of the boat so as not to halt his momentum. Then we're running left and right through bushes and around trees on a small path I no longer recognise.

He stops.

'Which way?'

'I'm not sure. I think we missed the turn back there.' I turn and run backwards the way we've just come. A gogo, balancing a pile of wood on her head, stares at us.

'*Sawubona*,' I start, between breaths.

'*Yebo*, Mama' – Siseko intervenes.

'*Yebo*.'

'*Ngapha?*'

She points to the right.

Siseko races down the path and I follow, aware that we've lost time. I keep following, disappointed that I'd missed the path and aware that Africa is language and people. As the writer Shaun Johnson says: 'Africa … is not a film set.'

As we reach the river, we drop the boat to the water and see that Simon and Craig have passed us while we were floundering in the bush and are already paddling a few hundred metres ahead down the river. We're disappointed but know our quest for gold is still very much alive.

As we pull out into the current, Loveday and Thando are next to us, having paddled around the Burma Road section. We chase the boat in front, gaining on them with every stroke. As we emerge, having shot the Pumphouse weir and rapid with aplomb, I allow my thoughts to drift back to the previous year's incident for the first time. I know now that – barring an extreme incident – I will get my tenth gold medal and Siseko will earn his first.

'Good driving!' I shout.

Approaching the finish, we feel tired but strong. Brad is on the bank.

'Well done, guys! Well done!'

The intensity of his pride in our achievement is tangible.

'Excellent, well done!' he shouts, running along the bank.

It's a wonderful feeling – there's a deep exhaustion from the three days' racing – but the crowd on the bank cheers and the satisfaction is enormous. As we approach the line, I see the nose of Loveday and Thando's boat inching up beside me. I respond and Siseko gives it all – and we're flying towards the finish line.

Seventh.

The moment is difficult to explain. All that's in my mind is the heat, the burning lungs and the ecstasy of the achievement. The injuries, challenges and hardships are all there, detailed away somewhere in my subconscious.

But they're not on my conscious mind. They contribute to the meaning of the moment.

Siseko turns, reaches a hand back, and our eyes meet as we hit hands. So much is meant but so little is said. We fall into the lagoon water, letting our bodies slowly cool down. Loveday, Thando, Siseko and me. I walk up the bank and hug Shelley with tears in my eyes. Brad's there, gathering us for photos and shouting the odds. Every second of the year's dedication and struggle is worth it for the next half an hour's satisfaction and contentment.

Movie Finish

Nearly three years later, I sit in a cinema chair watching Steve and Duma coming up to the finish line. They're paddling like mad, having just moved into tenth, ahead of their rivals Geoff and Eddie. The shot changes and we see them from the air. The spectators crowd the bank, cheering them on. They cross the line and Steve explodes with jubilation. They fall into the water, then turn and jump onto each other in a clinch. There's screaming and shouting as we see Dan 'Fish' and Oupa high-five each other and then come running to the water's edge and hugging the two champions. Steve looks at Annie and we know there's been an enormous amount of healing taking place. It's a beautiful moment. Steve and Duma get their gold medals from John Oliver right there on the bank in a moment of pure, blatant ecstasy that is obvious for anyone to see.

At first, it feels like it's completely over the top. But how do you communicate that feeling otherwise? That private moment of intrinsic satisfaction – which is made so sweet by the subconscious knowledge that a year of frustration, learning and focus, not to mention one and a half decades of commitment and effort, has finally triumphed – is impossible to translate. It's the same with Duma and his first time back in the boat with Steve earlier in the film – he's ecstatic.

The cinematography captures perfectly the passion and love for the sport that we enjoy, in such a way that a film audience can relate to it. Craig Freimond and Robbie Thorpe had a creative vision that captured so much *perfectly in the film. Grant Swanby, who plays the character Steve – who was originally based on me – and Lemogang Tsipa, who plays the re-interpreted Siseko, are brilliant on screen. Their dedication to looking authentic in the boat, their willingness to listen and share, and their ability to laugh made it a pleasure to be involved.*

PART 5

Dare to Dream

walk into the coffee shop, Europa, in Rosebank. A cursory glance around assures me neither Brad nor Ronnie are there yet. I sit and order a cappuccino. I can't help it with the smell of roasted beans in there. I've never met Ronnie but I've looked him up. The joys of Facebook and the internet. He's an incredibly successful guy. He was one of the original people to start Internet Solutions and made a fortune, I believe. Sounds like the sort of guy we need – to really make things happen.

My coffee comes and I start to sip quietly on my own, mulling things over in my head. Brad thinks there's a film in this story and I think there could be a great one. But what are the chances of it coming to light? It's a tough industry, we're led to believe. But then again, I've seen Brad beat the odds before. Light jazz plays and I wonder why I can never find the time to build a decent music collection. Or even just some music knowledge.

Then I see a guy who might be Ronnie walking in. 'A clever, Jewish boy,' my old colleague Sue had said. 'His mind works so fast, his words jam in his mouth because they can't get out fast enough.'

It's him.

'Hi, you must be Ronnie?' I stand and smile. He'd seemed pretty encouraging in his emails.

'Piers?'

'Yes, pleased to meet you. Hi.'

'Howzit.'

He sits down.

'I believe Brad's running a bit late.'

'Ja. I'm sure he won't be long.' I know he probably will, of course.

We sit there for a while, chatting about where each of us met Brad and what a great mate he is. And it's true what Sue said – about Ronnie speaking so fast. He's hungry and orders a sandwich. This guy talks fast, eats fast, moves fast.

After we've been carefully skirting the issue of the movie for about twenty minutes, Brad comes in smiling.

'Hey, Ronnie, Piers. Howzit!' Suddenly it's more relaxed. 'Sorry to keep you guys.'

'No problem. We were just chatting.'

Brad settles in and soon we get to the topic.

'So what did you think of the story?' he asks.

'Oh, ja, so tell me, Mike Mbanjwa won the Olympics?'

I'm completely taken aback. What's he talking about?

'What do you mean?' asks Brad. 'Did you read the speech?'

I'd delivered a speech at school about paddling the Dusi with Siseko. The theme had been 'perseverance' but we'd thought the more relevant themes for a movie might be more to do with black and white, old and young, working together. There were so many interesting sides to it. We thought.

'Sure, I read it. But what I'm saying is you've got to have a great story first.'

'Sure … but I think it is one.' I'm so glad Brad's on my team. I'm so bad at this type of difference of opinion.

'Okay, but you look at *Material*. I mean, that's a great story.' Ronnie was involved in writing and producing this very successful South African film.

'But hang on. This is a much better basic story than *Material*.' Brad's got that agitated expression on his face.

'What?'

Ronnie is incredulous. So is Brad. I sit there between them, thinking we're not off to a great start. I'm not sure what to say.

'Nearly 500 000 people saw *Material*,' Ronnie points out.

'Sure, I know it was great. All I'm saying is we've got the basics of a story as good as – if not better – here.'

Ronnie changes tack.

'Look, it does sound like an interesting story. But the industry's terrible. That old adage applies: Do you know how to make a small fortune in the film industry?' He barely pauses. 'Start with a big fortune. I know, I've seen it.'

The conversation between Brad and Ronnie carries on like this for a while.

'So you think it's a non-starter?' I venture a question.

'All I'm saying is this industry's tougher than anyone realises. Guys think they can throw a couple of million around and make a successful film. Let me tell you, it's not that easy.'

'We're not saying it's easy,' says Brad. 'We were just hoping you'd give us some tips. We really think it's a great story.'

'I appreciate that. But in all honesty, and I've been in this industry for ages, it's not worth it. It's a horrible place. Walk away. Guys just lose money in the film industry.'

'Did you see *Cool Runnings*?' Brad tries a different tack.

'Great film.'

'Exactly. Don't you think this could be something similar?'

'Maybe. … Mostly these projects aren't a success.'

'But we know that. We're not idiots.'

Brad looks at me. I wonder if perhaps we are. 'But if you never even give it a go, you've got no chance at all.'

'It's tough, Brad. It's tough. You've done so well. It's not worth it.'

'What about a documentary?' I feel like I'm watching a tennis match. I have to say something.

Ronnie just looks at me for a moment. 'A documentary?'

'Well, to us it was always a second prize,' I say. My father-in-law always says, 'Rather keep your mouth shut and let people think you're an idiot than open it – and remove all doubt.' I'm thinking I might have just removed any doubt.

'Most of those things are unwatchable!' Ronnie's adamant.

Brad smiles for a moment. He wants to make a feature film.

'What if you got a big star? Let's just say you got Charlize?' Brad tries. 'Or what if you got Gavin Hood to direct? A big star with a South African connection might just take it on out of social responsibility?'

'Brad, you're mad,' Ronnie shakes his head. 'I've spent time in Hollywood. Those big stars do nothing for nothing. They're business people. It's like … it's like you won't even get to talk to their agent. You won't even talk to their agent's agent!' he laughs.

'But come on, Ronnie, just give us a name then. Give us one guy in the industry we can talk to.'

'You need a story first.'

'We've got a story.'

'You may have part of a story. Someone has to write a script.'

'Okay, so then we get someone to write a script.'

'There are only a few guys in the country who can actually do that. And you're talking a fair amount of money already. It can take years. Just understand, you're talking about R300 000 to R400 000 just for a script,' Ronnie says. I sigh.

'And then you've only got a piece of intellectual material,' he carries on. 'You need to invest up to half a million rand in a piece of intellectual material. Then there are still no guarantees. Then you run around trying to sell that piece of intellectual material to someone who wants to invest another ten or so million in a movie. Who in their right mind wants to invest their millions in a movie? Do you know how few movies actually make any money? Very few. Very, very few.'

Brad's getting irritated. 'Who's the best guy to write a script for us?'

But Ronnie just shakes his head, 'You're going to waste your time and money. Trust me, I know.'

We chat about other things, pay the bill and leave. I walk away under the paperbark trees feeling pretty deflated. It's not really what we were hoping for. Still, I think, the best way to get Brad to do something is to tell him it can't be done.

A week later, we sit at the same table. This time, it's me, Brad and

Robbie Thorpe. It seems Ronnie's come round and given Brad a contact. I suspect it might have been just to get him off his back, but who cares? Here we are at least.

'You won't find a more inspired storytelling mind than Robbie,' Ronnie had said in his email. And Robbie certainly looks like he could be in the film industry, I think. Longish dishevelled hair, and a purple-patterned, long-sleeved shirt. He speaks like a bit of a hippie but he can't hide his interest.

'What a great story!' he kicks off.

Wow. I nearly fall off my chair.

Brad just smiles. 'You think so, Robbie?'

'Sure. I loved the speech. It's moving.'

'Really?' I ask.

'Sure. In fact, it's got many of the elements you need for a film to be a success.' I'm not sure if this guy's having us on or if he really thinks that. Then he puts me squarely in my place:

'The only thing was, just when you should have hit the climax, you kind of let it fall down.'

I smile knowingly, but there are too many thoughts in my head for me to really think clearly about what he's just said.

'You don't think we should be thinking of making a documentary?' Brad asks.

'Well, you must decide. Do you want to make a documentary? Or do you want to make a feature film? You know, I don't know, what are your objectives?'

'What we really set out to do was tell a story we thought might be good for our sport, possibly other sports, and maybe, if we really push it, for it be a story that would be good for South Africa.' Finally, I feel like I'm contributing to the conversation.

'It's a story that definitely needs to be told,' Robbie agrees. 'And we're desperate for stories like this at the moment.'

'Exactly,' agrees Brad. 'We just thought that a documentary might be cheaper. We might have more of a chance getting the story out there.'

'I'm not saying you can't do both. But how many people watch a documentary? Nearly half a million people watched *Material* in total.'

'Wow.' Brad's impressed.

So am I, but didn't Ronnie already tell us that?

'If you want to make a documentary, by all means, go ahead. But I think this thing's got huge cinematic potential.'

Brad and I just smile at each other. So we weren't just dreaming; we weren't so far off the mark.

'Look,' says Robbie, 'Ronnie's right. It's a tough industry. Things don't just come easy. And most projects don't see the big screen; he was right about that too. And he was right about another thing: you need the right team. I'd love to be involved, and I've got just the right guy to write your script. But we're going to be busy on another project for at least a year. But you've got to decide if you want to give it a go.'

Two hours later, after enthusing about all of the potential and opportunities around our big dream, we walk out through the doors and through the paperbark trees – in the belief that, if we sit patiently for a year, something great might happen.

That evening, I'm paddling on the dam and head over to Siseko. I tell him about the idea of making a film and he's pretty upbeat.

'Maybe it can help some people, Piers.'

'That's exactly what we're hoping.'

'Especially if the guys can see where I come from.'

'Ja?'

'Maybe then they can see that you can come from the townships and still get somewhere with your life.'

'Exactly.'

In that moment, the vision of SCARC, the movie, everything, all seems so clear to me. We pick the pace up and paddle for another 45 minutes while the sun drops and the cool breeze picks up over the water.

A week later, Brad and I meet with Craig Freimond and Robbie Thorpe. They're fired up about making this movie. It all seems to have swivelled around and we can't quite work out how.

'So what's changed?' Brad asks. 'After last week, we had our minds set on waiting a year for the team to assemble.'

'Well, things have changed,' Robbie says. 'That project's actually fallen through.'

Much later, we learn why. Craig and Robbie had been working on a film around race and reconciliation that was to feature Trevor Noah. Unfortunately, the project never really worked and then, at a critical moment, Trevor had picked up his role on the American news satire and talk show *The Daily Show*. It was an incredible opportunity for him, and, it turns out, for us too. Garth Japhet, CEO of the NGO Heartlines, had been working with Craig and Robbie on the project for a while. They had managed to garner impressive investment for the concept and now they were literally sitting up the proverbial creek without a paddle. Garth, a qualified medical doctor turned social upliftment entrepreneur, had been working on this concept of: 'I know your name, but not your story' for years. How pertinent that theme is for the place our country is at, we thought. And our story would perfectly exemplify their values. Garth would later say that the coincidence was nothing short of miraculous.

Inspired by Real Events

When you go to the cinema, a film that's 'inspired by real events' or 'based on a true story' might be exactly that. And no more. One thing we were to realise pretty soon as we embarked on this journey was that if we were to achieve our original goals – to broaden the awareness of the sport we loved, to inspire people with a South African success story and to tell people about a model that we believed could be successful – it would be important that the film-makers be given the space to tell a story that people would want to hear that would also work on screen. Ronnie Apteker might have given us a tough baptism, but he'd certainly put us in touch with the right crew. Together Robbie and Craig would create a story that – when we finally watched – we thought would be a great success. But it was as if they had to teach us to jump through a few hoops first.

About twelve months, around 120 emails to Craig and about eight hours of interviews later, I'm at my desk at work while Robbie and Craig are away on some kind of work trip, 'workshopping' the story, when my phone rings. It's Robbie. I answer.

'Howzit, Piers?' He always sounds so laid-back, as if he's on the beach or something.

We chat about how things are going before he gets to the point.

'So Piers, I'm just phoning to tell you about our first challenge on this project.'

'Yes …' I reply hesitantly.

'So we've got these two main characters.'

'Yes …'

'And what we're finding is the character based on Siseko, the young black guy … as we're thinking of depicting him in the film …' It sounds to me like he's stalling and I start to get nervous … 'Well, he's really interesting and he's got this tough background. And that sets him up for a journey.'

'Sure, that sounds about right.'

'And then we've got your character.'

'Ja?'

'Well, we need him to go through some kind of growth in order for the audience to identify with him.'

'Okay.' Now I have no idea where this is going at all.

'So he needs to start as a "broken character" in some way or another so that he can really grow through the process.'

'Right.'

And then I start to see where he's going.

'Don't take this the wrong way, but basically what I'm trying to tell you is you're just too boring to make a movie out of …'

And he starts to laugh. It's one of those warm-up laughs while you hope the other guy will also start to laugh quite soon. I start to laugh, but it's a nervous kind of laugh.

'So, look,' he carries on, 'don't panic, but wait and see what we come up with. But I'm just telling you so that you can prepare yourself.'

'Thanks.'

'Remember that we want you guys all to feel a part of this process as we go. We don't want you to feel unhappy about the direction the project takes at any point. We want everyone who's on board to be working towards the final vision.'

'No Eeyores,' I say.

Robbie calls nay-sayers – people who struggle to focus on the positives – 'Eeyores' after the melancholic character in Winnie the Pooh.

'Exactly. No Eeyores.'

We chat a bit longer and then eventually we hang up. I'm not exactly sure what just happened, but I feel a little deflated.

About a month later, I'm summoned to a meeting with all the major stake-holders in the film. Siseko, Brad and I sit at one end of the table, wondering how the project has progressed. Craig and Robbie go through the laborious process of explaining to us how they've needed to make some changes to the story in order for it to work as a film script. Garth and the Heartlines team are there. Garth reassures us that they want us to be a part of the process. Then Robbie makes the point that my life is great but that it's not that interesting in terms of cinematic value. I know this. Then they get into describing how they see the film plot panning out. Robbie takes the lead:

'So what we thought would work well is if Siseko's character, Duma, begins as a criminal.'

I look across at Siseko – our second-year Law student. He doesn't flinch.

'He's a complex character,' Robbie continues. 'He's at a crossroads in his life, where he's going to be forced to make some tough choices.' Robbie's looking fairly concerned. 'He starts out as a criminal, he's caught up with stealing cable with a friend of his. Then later on he's drawn into the paddling, where he finds success and, through that, he has the opportunity to build a different, but in some ways, tougher life for himself.'

'You'll obviously have to make it pretty clear that Siseko was never a real criminal because he's studying Law?' I pose this more as a question than as a statement. I'm beginning to worry about what they might have done to make my character 'interesting'.

'I think there are ways of making the distinction between characters and the real people on which they're based.' Craig's spent a lot more time with Siseko and me and he takes the opportunity to reassure us at this point. 'And we have some ideas around that which we'll share with you later.'

Siseko nods. He's cool. That's one thing for sure about Siseko, I think – he's cool.

'Carrying on from that,' Robbie continues, 'with your character, Piers.'

I look up.

'We needed the character to make an equally significant journey through the course of the film.'

'Ja?' I think about my life for a moment. I have a great life. I love teaching. I have a wonderful wife and two fantastic children. I feel privileged to have enjoyed some great experiences. But I'm as surprised as anyone else that there's a film being made that involves my life.

'In order for him to do that, and for the audience to really relate to him, we need him to be a broken character at the start. So what we've done is we've made him lose a son at the start ...'

Suddenly, the world seems quiet. I have never felt so conspicuous in my life. I can feel sweat beads forming on my forehead. It feels like I'm only just balancing on my chair. Brad turns to me, lifts his eyebrows and half smiles. 'Wow, good luck,' he seems to say.

'Um ... okay, that's um ...' I trail off and nod thoughtfully instead.

'But listen,' Garth chimes in again, 'we would never allow any part of this process to upset you or Siseko. We want this to be a journey we take together. In any case, we'd benefit from having you guys involved throughout the process. I mean we foresee a role for you in somehow marketing the film at the end.'

It feels like there's a lot of repetition going on from where I'm sitting.

'Sure ...'

I'm not sure what else to say. The room is still very, very quiet.

'I mean, an idea like that takes some getting used to.'

The meeting bandies about a bit and then winds up. I walk out, not too sure what just happened in there, but by that evening, there's already an enormous and overwhelming sense of ... relief. This is no longer my story. I'll be divorced from the story from that point on. I can contribute to the story without having to always make comparisons with what really happened.

A while later, I've become friends with the film director Craig Freimond and we end up hashing out a conversation that I'll have with many other people.

'There's something I can never quite put my finger on,' I start.

'What's that?'

'Why us?'

'What do you mean?'

'Why is the movie about us?

'Your guys' story fits the whole concept of what we're trying to do here. It's a story we desperately need to hear.'

'Sure, I get that. But Martin Dreyer and Thulani Mbanjwa won the race together back in 2008. Andy and S'bonelo won together in 2014. There are definitely more successful black-and-white partnerships than ours. The best marathon paddler in the world, Hank McGregor, lives in South Africa.'

'So?'

'They've got amazing stories to tell.'

'I'm sure they do.' Craig looks at me for a while, shrugs. 'But we're telling your story.'

And it'll be a journey I'll love.

Returning to the Koppie

Light is just beginning to infiltrate the smudgy darkness of the previous night. I lock the car and turn away from the park. Already, the catering team are setting up tables and chairs where the film crew will enjoy a hearty cooked breakfast in an hour's time. And cheap coffee, I smile.

Slowly, I start jogging towards the gate. The sandy pathway is knobbly with stones and small rocks under my shoes. The rhythm of a trail runner is totally different from that of the road runner. You're completely alert, eyes fixed on the path ahead, constantly processing information, planning your route, with your proprioception responding to each footfall. It's been a while since I have run here. Sometimes, you just have to do things without thinking too much about it, though. They say it's about getting back on the horse. I suppose I was scared that if I thought too much about it, I wouldn't make it. So here I am, running the Melville koppies. Up to this point this morning, my actions have been mechanical and methodical. I feel as if I've been going through the motions while almost looking the other way. A forced avoidance. But the moment I'm through the gate, things are different. Now I'm not just an alert trail runner, my senses are on edge. A dusky bulbul chirrup-chirps me from a gnarled acacia branch as I run quietly beneath it. I make my way towards the top of the ridge. Along the rocky outcrop, I meander towards the highest point. From here you can look out over much of Johannesburg. To the east, the city cuts a famous silhouetted skyline in front of the sunrise. To the north, the suburbs undulate gracefully away. The largest man-made forest, they call it. But there are a full 360 degrees' worth of views here. It's not a patch on Sydney, Cape Town or other beautiful cities, I think. But this view is an asset to the city – and totally wasted. Few people come here. Aside from the Zionists, who gather at sacred prayer sites early on Sunday mornings, their white cassocks striking a clean circle against the rocky slopes.

I run down the first ledge and past the site of the miserable incident. There's nothing to distinguish it. A scrappy patch of dirt and stones. But Gav and I won't forget it. Ever. I stare for a while then carry on along the path, thinking of very little. Then I feel glad to have come here to run again – even if it might only be for the last time. I follow the path down the second ledge. It's the rockiest section – big steps – and, as you dip down, the trees create a tidy indigenous canopy. A hadeda takes off from behind a rock, almost under my feet – screeching 'wah, wah, wahaha' – and frightens the living daylights out of me. My heart races and sweat beads emerge in a split second on my forehead. A few adrenaline-infused minutes of running later, I laugh at myself – closure takes time, they say. I run for another half an hour on my old routes on the koppies, then head back to the top where they're doing the shoot today.

Paddling at Orlando

Steve Andrews, middle aged, some say 'over the hill', dark-haired and serious, leaves his Land Rover parked where the dusty road ends. He's completely out of sorts here ...

•

But at least he's there ... I've spent many days on set watching the filming process. Although laborious and repetitive at times, I've found it fascinating. I never visited Siseko when he lived in the settlement. Soon after we started paddling together, he moved into the house that became the 'SCARC digs'. Brad had bought a house to allow some of the guys to live closer to work, Emmarentia Dam and their tertiary institutions – as usual, generous to an extreme. Yes, I'd picked him up from the digs and dropped him off there many times, but there would have been something expressed in visiting him in the informal settlement. As I sit there, watching the shoot, the technology and equipment used by the film crew and their professional behaviour and communication are a contrast to the lackadaisical atmosphere, the dust and squalor of the township.

'It's a wrap,' Craig shouts.

Every film set finishes with the same words and a minor celebration.

I chat and linger for a moment in the knowledge that this is the only time in my life I will likely be a part of the film-making process. Soon after that, I turn to walk to my car.

As I'm pulling off to head back home, I look across at Orlando Dam. I think of the beginnings of the journey for the SCARC club and the drowning of Luzuko, and then I think of a small boy travelling from the Eastern Cape. I think of the importance of birth certificates and the mystery of the mountain.

It's 4.30pm on a Wednesday. The youngsters will probably be training on Orlando Dam. So I turn left instead of right and wind my way round behind the back of the cooling towers to Power Park. I drive among the sturdy houses of the suburb, following the road grid. Then I turn off the tar and on to the dirt road that leads to the dam. There seems to be a burst water pipe or something because there's water drifting down the road in a small but persistent stream. I open the window to be greeted by the powerful and unmistakeable stench of sewerage. This is unbelievable. I see a bunch of the SCARC guys on the bank, waiting to paddle, it seems. As I pull up, Sipho is the first to greet me.

'Hey, howzit, Piers?'

They're all clearly surprised to see me. I don't paddle in Soweto very often – three or four times ever.

'Howzit, guys. What's happening with the water quality?'

'The water quality?'

'How long has this broken pipe been pouring into the dam?'

'Maybe ... one or two weeks now. But at first it was not so bad.'

They don't seem too perturbed. I'm horrified.

'Are you still training here?'

'Sorry?'

'Are you guys still training here, with the pipe leak?'

'Ja. We're still training here.'

I climb out of the car. The guys are so pleased to see me.

'Are you joining us for the session?' a young guy whose name I can't quite remember asks. His eyes are more than hopeful – imploring.

'I'd planned on it,' is the best I can manage, still looking for a way out.

I'm hoping I can convince them not to get on because of what seems to me to be a major sewerage leak. Then Thando pipes up:

'We're doing nine down to two, one-minute rest between intervals.'

He's talking about the session they plan on doing: paddle hard for nine minutes, easy for one minute, then paddle hard for eight minutes and so on. It's a fairly tough session.

'Has anyone phoned to report this leak?' I'm trying to get back to the main issue on my mind.

'We've phoned in twice. Actually, Nkosi's phoned twice. But you know these guys.'

'Come, let's get going,' says Thando.

I'm starting to think there's no option.

'Have none of you guys got sick from this water?'

No one answers me. The guys are starting to get changed, some are picking up their boats and heading for the water already. So I walk to the back of my car and start to change for the session. Looks like this *umlungu* is going to have to suck it up.

Minutes later, I'm kitted out and carrying my boat to the water's edge. The contrast on the senses is a complete overload ... The sun sits above a koppie, reflecting off the water – beautiful! The weavers and bishop birds cling to bulrushes as they swing in the wind – beautiful. I step lightly over an Omo packet to get to the water's edge. The smell starts to cling to me. My skin itches, my mouth is firmly closed as I paddle away from the bank. For the first time in my life, I hope the guys will speak isiZulu or isiXhosa so that I won't have to answer.

The session is tough. Impressive, even. Thando is in good shape and keen to flex his muscles. The younger guys start the intervals too hard and then fade – but by then they've already set the tone for the interval. I spend the session trying to avoid water splashed from paddle blades reaching my face. The water on my arms feels cool in the breeze, but sticky. As we finish the session, I'm off the water as quickly as possible but the guys linger afterwards, wanting to chat.

'Hey, Piers, what do you think of these Gara paddles?' a youngster asks.

'Ja, they're good paddles. That shape is good for sprints.'

'For sprints?'

'It catches well at the front of the stroke.'

'I think I can be fast with this paddle.'

'You must try to find what works for you. Try different things.'

I wonder how easy it is for these guys to find access to different types of equipment. I look at some of their paddles. There are plenty of worn paddles – some must be 2 centimetres shorter than when they were new.

'Okay guys, I must get going.'

'Cool, you should come here sometimes.'

'You're right. It's great. Just that it's far.' That's the truth too. 'Listen, I'm going to phone about this sewerage leak. The guys must fix it, otherwise it's going to stop us being able to paddle here.'

As I say this, I know I won't be coming here to paddle until this water problem is completely sorted out. The guys still linger, chatting a little, and I think of Siseko telling me how he kept coming back to the dam because it gave him 'something useful to do in the afternoons'.

By the time I'm in my car, they're walking back up the road in small groups, dwarfed by the giant cooling towers. Meandering. I drive up the dirt track, through the small stream flowing towards the dam, then turn on to the tar road, give a last wave and leave them walking up the slope behind me.

Later that night, I phone Brad and tell him about the water problem. I phone Jo'burg Water, sit on hold for fifteen minutes and then listen to five minutes of information on water stations for areas without water. Eventually, I speak to a young man who expresses real concern. He gives me a reference number and I hang up.

Two days later, Nkosi tells me the problem persists. The stream keeps flowing. So I write an email explaining that there will be filming happening at the dam the following week. That there will be press there, actors, celebrities even! I hear nothing. I forward my email to Brad, who forwards it to Nomsa, the secretary of Andile Ramaphosa. The problem is officially fixed at 10pm that Saturday night.

Shoot in the Valley

I turn my alarm off at 4.30am. Again. We've been filming continuously now for over a week. The film crew seems to be tired and I can see why. I'm quickly through the shower and out into the corridor. Through the glass hotel doors, I see some of the camera guys milling around. Red Bull and cigarettes for breakfast. I'm not sure how they do it. I certainly don't know how sustainable it is.

'Hey, Piers!'

Brad joined us the previous afternoon by way of a flight from Johannesburg and a taxi through the Valley of a Thousand Hills to Dusi Bridge. That must be a first, I think.

'Hey, Fish. How's it going?'

'Ja, good. Quite exciting to be here.'

Later, we're eating breakfast with the crew. The hierarchical lines are pretty strict on set. You only sit at the director's table if you're a producer, main actor or the director of photography. Everyone else steers clear, doing their best to look busy.

Brad had been the original initiator of the film. I thought it was a fantastic idea but wasn't sure it would have the legs to go all the way. Siseko and I had paddled down a river because we wanted to. For both of us, it was the best chance at a good result. We'd had some awesome experiences along the way and people on the side seemed to think it was a great story, But here we are now, with a big budget – by South African standards – behind us, halfway through making a film.

On the way into the Dusi valley for the first shoot of the morning, Brad insists on stopping and buying us a good cup of coffee from a local café. The catering on set has been spectacular – the only exception being that the coffee's cheap and not so cheerful. In keeping with the hierarchy, a tray of take-away cappuccinos from the local Wimpy arrives for the directors and producers. But for the rest of us it's Ricoffy or nothing. Or in our case: buy your own. This brief intermission leaves us trailing the eighteen-car entourage into the valley and out of sight. The drive into the Valley of a Thousand Hills from Cato Ridge is spectacular. The road is windy and steep. Wisps of mist hang in the valley. Uncountable houses, many of them makeshift, dot the green-and-ochre rolling hills that stretch to the horizon. I often think of the early pioneers of the race, in a lonely valley seeing only a couple of local people in their non-stop, week-long journey to the sea.

By the time we get down to Dusi Bridge, there's a paramedic car trailing us – they've obviously also stopped along the way. But as we pull up at the bridge, there are no cars in sight and certainly no hired trucks carrying tons of equipment.

'Great. I thought you said we were meeting at Dusi Bridge?' I ask.

'I never said Dusi Bridge,' Brad responds. 'You said Craig told you Dusi Bridge.'

'No, man. You said when we stopped for coffee, that we'd catch them at Dusi Bridge.'

I check my phone for the daily schedule but I've left it on airplane mode and when I turn it back on the signal's sketchy and the emails don't seem to be coming through. Before we allow the situation to deteriorate into an argument, I'm on my phone, trying to call the producer, Robbie. But his phone goes straight to voice mail. They're obviously out of range. I try Craig but have the same problem. We talk to the paramedics but they say they were following us because they thought we knew where we were going.

'How many times have you done this race?' the driver asks. I tell him I know the route by river but he just looks at me.

'Great,' I say again. 'The shoot starts in twenty minutes.'

We decide to follow the river by road to the next obvious point, which would be the Saddles portage area. The paramedic car bounces comically along the dirt road behind us. The views of the river down to our left as we bumble along are beautiful, but I'm in no mood to admire them. I've been overly conscious of not appearing to take any liberties throughout the filming process.

In the passenger seat next to me, Brad reclines the seat and falls asleep. Clearly, he's not stressed.

We come to a T-junction in the road and I guess left. A few minutes later, a cluster of vehicles emerges, nestled into a dip in the valley. Fantastic! Relief. I'm whisked off to 'make-up' while Brad still sleeps in the car.

The 'make-up caravan' is a lot less glamorous than in Hollywood. I sit on a plastic chair under a pop-up gazebo looking at the acacia trees while Bronwyn hunches over me, applying sticky black dye to my hair.

'This one sticks a lot better than the one we used the other day,' she informs me. 'It shouldn't run even if you're on the water.'

'Fantastic,' I retort. 'I presume that means it doesn't come out easily in the shower either?'

For some reason, I hate the stiffness of hair product in my hair and she chuckles at me. The first hair dye they'd used had started rinsing out as they filmed me paddling in the river. The 'continuity team' thought it was a dead give-away. But the second type they found would really stick. The only drawback was that later I'd look at the bottom of the shower and see this seething mass of soapy black foam.

Grant Swanby, the actor playing the character who was originally based on me, has dark almost black hair tinged with grey. They've dyed the grey black and now they're dying my hair much darker so that I can play the 'body double' for 'myself'. The idea was for me to do any of the paddling scenes that involved paddling through rapids as well as any of the tougher scenes running with the boat where my face need not be shot close-up on camera. Once one understands that the actors need to protect their careers, one starts to respect the need for them to have 'stunt doubles' for even the most tame action shots. If an actor breaks his leg –

and is in a cast for a few weeks – that can easily put him out of playing a role, and possibly several months' income. It could also jeopardise the entire film.

Having said that, however, Grant and Lemo won my absolute respect with the commitment they made in trying to look authentic in the boat. Learning to paddle a racing K1 or K2 is like learning to ride a bicycle for the first time. It happens quickly if you're five years old and have a low centre of gravity, but if you're 35 or 45, it normally takes a good six months. Getting to a competitive level – the level Grant and Lemo had to try and portray for the film – can take even the most talented athletes years to accomplish. They'd had three months.

One of the scenes being shot this morning is a portaging scene up a steep dirt jeep track. When Craig calls for extra actors needed to portray the boats being overtaken by the 'heroes', Brad and I jump at the opportunity. Just being involved in the shooting is a lot of fun. Craig explains that the idea is that the main actors are on a roll, cutting through the field while their competition looks on exhausted and unable to respond to their pace … So we're 'costumed up' to be competitors, so that the main characters can come flying past us on a hill as they make their way towards the top ten.

We line up at the bottom of the steep hill with a boat on our shoulders just in front of Grant and Lemo. At Craig's instruction, we start walk-jogging up the hill. As they start to pass us, I feel a distinctive 'push' from behind as Brad's competitive instinct kicks in. I can read his mind: no pair of 'pretentious actors' is going to have an easy time passing him up a hill carrying a boat. No matter what the director's instructions are! Grant and Lemo respond by running harder to get past us. I concentrate on keeping Brad at bay and trying to let them succeed – all the time trying to look exhausted and frustrated. But, before long, we're running too. They eventually make it past.

'Shouldn't there be more jostling and pushing as they come past?' Brad asks Craig at the top.

'Well, what's it really like?'

'The guys don't make it easy, that's for sure.'

'You'd stay on the path and make them come around you,' I say, 'but you wouldn't try and push them into the bush. Very few guys would do that.'

'Okay, let's try again and see how it goes. Make it difficult for them, but, I mean, remember they're the heroes – they must get past,' Craig smiles.

Soon we're back at the bottom of the hill and starting again. I can see Grant and Lemo looking determined. Trevor's got the camera and he's racing backwards up the hill, trying to keep it as steady as he can. He's got a gaggle of crew helpers all bustling about him at the same time. It can't be easy.

As we start, Brad's pushing like crazy and, before I know it, we're moving at surprising speed up the hill. Grant and Lemo are half sprinting, half scrambling in the mud and gravel to get past. There's a lunge to the left and, as I glance back, I see Brad has given Grant a bit of a shoulder nudge. He looks more than a little surprised. They pick up their pace even more and mud flies from under their shoes as they 'rev into the red' to get ahead. I chuckle to myself. It'd be almost impossible to run up a hill this fast in the race but I'm hoping it'll look good on camera – at least give people an idea of how competitive and gruelling the race can be.

At the top, I'm sucking for air. It's always humid as hell in the valley. But I'm loving it. I look at Lemo and he's tired but enjoying it too, I think. Brad's sweating and puffing but he's got a slight smile on his face. Then I look at Grant. He's doubled over and gripping his calf muscle. His face is white.

The paramedics are there in a flash and before long Grant's diagnosed with a serious muscle strain, possibly a minor tear. That's not good news at all. Craig has every right to be annoyed, but if he is he's hiding it well. Brad's all smiles. I think he thinks these actors need to get the proper feel of how tough the race is anyway. I'm not too upset if it means they need to use me more as the double because, frankly, I'm loving being involved.

Fortunately, the next shoot's a paddling one. Our eighteen-car entourage snakes through the valley to below the confluence with the Umgeni, all the way to Gauging weir. Craig and Trevor are after a shot from below the weir with the boats coming towards the camera – and it sounds great to me. It's an extraordinary thing to be a film director. Craig has the ability to think creatively in every aspect of the film – whether he's behind the camera with Trevor, or having a quiet word with one of the actors. He's also got a way of sharing his vision with people in a way that makes them want to be a part of it. He's brought his team down into one of the most remote parts of the Dusi valley. The pool of water is banked by boulders at least 100 metres high and it makes for a pretty spectacular setting. While the crew's eating lunch, Brad and I paddle our K1s around on the pool above the weir and by the time they call us and tell us to move out of the shot, we've got in a pretty good session. Gauging weir spans about 50 metres across. On a full level, it's a pretty impressive sight to see the mighty expanse of water crashing through. Competent paddlers shoot the weir fairly regularly but it's temperamental. Occasionally it bares its vicious teeth and smashes a boat.

'Guys shoot this thing all the time,' Brad shouts to Craig.

'Really?'

'Sure, I've shot it a few times.'

'That might look great,' Trevor chips in.

'Okay, let's get some of these extras to shoot it first and see how it goes.'

I can see Craig's not convinced. He's got one actor with a strained calf muscle already. They're stable on flat water but shooting a weir is another story.

The young guys chosen to shoot the weir seem up for it though and moments later they're set in concentration and skimming across the pool towards us. I wonder briefly if their line is too straight as they go over the weir. You need to shoot it at around 45 degrees to avoid the risk of hitting the submerged wall under the white water. It's an impressive sight as they accelerate over the weir with the power of the falling water. The stopper wave crashes over the front paddler's head and he's completely gone from view for a moment before there's a loud crack. The boat stops dead and bounces up with the front metre of the nose pointing at the sky.

'Oh shit.'

'Perhaps you could keep your suggestions to a minimum from now on, Brad?' pipes Craig.

Any Given Thursday

There's an American football film called *Any Given Sunday*. The title emphasises the passion for the sport of the fans and players and how, throughout the season, the football games will go ahead on every Sunday. The Thursday night 'time trial' at Emmarentia Dam has a similar culture. If Christmas day falls on a Thursday, there might not be an official dice, but otherwise it's a sure bet. A time trial, by definition, in other sports means each individual setting off on their own and trying to cover a set distance in as fast a time as possible. For us, it's a misnomer. It's not a time trial at all.

It's a ten-lap mass start race around the buoys which skirt Emmarentia Dam in a 1-kilometre loop. There are three tight turns every lap, where the boats converge and compete in what can sometimes be termed mayhem. Without exaggeration. By the third or fourth lap, slower boats are already being lapped by the faster bunches and, to complicate matters further, there are separate starts, one and three minutes apart for the K1s, K2s and K3s. One of South Africa's most versatile and successful paddlers – and an Olympian too – Mark Perrow described it as the best place in the world to learn racing strategy and tactics. There was a time when the standard of paddling there was so high, few would have argued.

One Thursday evening in March, when the weather is at its best for paddling – not the searing heat of summer, nor the hand-numbing chill of highveld winters – I warm up with a couple of easy laps. It's after the Dusi and also the Umkomaas canoe marathons and I'm feeling fit and strong. I think of Tennyson, 'though much is taken … much abides'. I'm half serious, half joking. Fighting wars in the world of ancient Greek mythology is a little different from paddling round the pond. But then sportsmen and women are the post-modern gladiators, aren't they? Sort of.

We line up, rudders against the banks, waiting for the siren to signal the start. A good start's essential as around 50 boats will race 500 metres to a single buoy where, from flatout 20-odd kilometres an hour, they will slow in order to make a near 180-degree turn. After that, the dam water becomes a sloppy, choppy mess. Get stuck at the back of the bunch and, unless you've got some serious horsepower left in the tank, you're out the back door.

I'm lined up on the far right. The shorter line to the buoy, but the water's shallower on that side. It's harder to paddle in shallow water – the boat feels heavier. It's much of a muchness wherever you start from. I look across to the left. The low sun glints on the club windows on the far side of the dam. There are a few SCARC guys who are contenders to keep me off the front bunch – Siyabonga, Alex, Zonele maybe. There are a few others who might be up there, but Wayne and the Hamster are in a K2. Thank goodness. And then there's Siseko. He'll either take the lead from the start and have us strung out, scratching to stay on his wave by the first buoy, or he'll hang back and let us sort out the pecking order before taking command later on. He's in a different league and can pretty much do as he pleases. The last boats are in line. We wait. A boat creeps forward on the far left. It's Tex. Once one starts, the rest follow. The line moves forward gradually, some more brazen than others.

The siren. Power into the water and we're off. Four long, hard strokes and then pick up the rate. After twenty strokes, I'm flying. Thirty strokes and I'm virtually at top speed. I look across to the left. Siseko's about a boat length in front. Impressive. I put my head down and keep powering for another ten strokes and then start drifting to the left, hoping to get to his wave. I look up – he's going 'balls to the wall', flat-out, and I'm losing ground. I guide the nose of my boat towards his wave, my heart rate climbing and my breathing coming harder and harder. I get to the wave but there's no let up. He really is giving it to us.

Siyabonga's on the left side and there's a boat behind me, also to the left, but I can't look back. It's taking everything I've got just to hold the wave. Approaching the buoy, Siseko accelerates once more and I feel the nose start to come up. Then, rounding the buoy, he lets up. Thank the Pope. Some relief. He pulls steadily to the top buoy, keeping us working, but at least we're not in the red. Around the clubhouse buoy, Siyabonga goes to the front. Zonele is with us but he takes his time getting round to the inside. He's a great natural athlete but he's not fit enough to play in this pen at the moment. Siyabonga puts the hammer down and I have to scramble across to the inside wave, leaving the diamond open for Zonele – if he can get there. He does. These young boys can accelerate, I think. They're so light. Siyabonga tears past the Scout Hall, making me work – but not into the red zone. Not quite. He pulls like that all the way down to the bottom buoy. He slows round the buoy and Siseko surprises us completely by going to the front again. I'm quick getting up on to his wave, though. I'm 41 – I need to be.

He ups the ante until we're going flat out again. Red-lining it all the way to the buoy. I know I can't do this for another ten laps, but I've learned to believe that the other guys can't either. You have to believe it, otherwise you're out. I look across at Zonele – he looks worse than I feel, if that's possible. At the club, Siseko eases up, forcing me to take the pull. But I'm on the inside and I use his bow wave to turn my boat for me. I get in four recovery strokes. I look left. The guys are 'faffing', taking their time. So I hit it hard. As hard as I can. I put myself way over the edge for maybe 30 strokes. I look back. Zonele's off the wave – caught by surprise and floundering. Siyabonga's just on the wave, but far back. About to fall off. I keep going for another twenty strokes, which takes us around the Scout Hall buoy. I turn hard left and pick up the tail wave of a K3 in front of us. It surfs my boat for four strokes and the speed picks up. Perfect luck. I look back. Siyabonga's off the wave. If I can hold it to the buoy, they might throw in the towel. So I hang in.

I glance briefly to my right to see Siseko sitting comfortably on the wave. Annoying. I think he's even breathing through his nose! I hold my pace as best I can for the rest of the lap. When I look back, we've got a 50-metre lead. Fantastic. Siseko takes the pull at the end of the lap. I'm at his mercy. He picks the pace up again. I'm staying on his wave – but only just. It feels like 'the amount that will kill me minus one'.

By the time he's pulled a lap, we've opened a significant gap on the guys behind us. I'm having to paddle at my limit to stay with him, but then I pull a lap again. I recover slightly but try to keep the pace reasonable so that Siseko sees some value in having me there. We alternate like this all the way through to the end of the eighth lap. I'm at my limit on Siseko's wave as he pulls and then I try to limit the damage on mine. But he's recovering on my wave enough to be fresh for his pulls.

By the start of the ninth lap, I'm seriously exhausted. It's already dark. I look at the clock, squinting against the spotlight above the club: 36:50. It's fast. If we can paddle the last two laps at an average of 4:35 each, we can dip under 46 minutes. It's possible, but it'll be a stretch. My best time prior to this is 46:15. Definitely on the cards. Unbelievable. In that moment, there are splinters of thoughts submerged into my subconscious by my tired but focused brain. There's something about a personal best time at 41 years old. And there's something about being the last man left on Siseko's wave while he drops the rest of the field in his wake. The young ex-protégé helps out the old bull? But the job's not done. Not yet. Not quite. I pull as hard as I can for a lap, knowing we're almost done. I look up to my right: 41:30. The best I can do. But too slow. We need a 4:30 lap now to get under 46. It's up to Siseko. And will I even be able to hang on? I hope briefly that he won't hold back and keep something in reserve for the end sprint. As if he needs to.

'Go for 46 minutes,' I squeeze out.

He does.

All through that lap, I hold on to the wave. By the proverbial ball hair. He gives me space around the boats we're lapping and just enough water – no more – to get my nose around the last buoy. Approaching the finish, the idea of sprinting is preposterous. I'm already sprinting just to be there.

I just try to stay on his wave. It's too hard. I almost vomit with the effort. But somehow I'm still there. It's so hard that I hate the sport.

We cross the line: 45:55. I'm ecstatic. I'm in love with the sport. I'm breathing so hard that I can't thank Siseko. I look across. But I don't have to say anything. He knows.

Acknowledgements

I would like to thank my family, most importantly my wife, Shelley, for her patience and support and especially for the many years of seconding. Thanks also to my biggest fans, Emma and Dominic.

Thank you to my editor, Craig Higginson, for his understanding and guidance. Thanks also to the Pan Macmillan team, in particular, Andrea Nattrass, Nkateko Traore, Eileen Bezemer and Terry Morris, for their enthusiasm for my book.

For advice and reflection on my writing, I thank Nic Oldert and Craig Freimond.

For the many hours of interviews, I am grateful to Nkosi Mzolo, Ryno Armdorf and Siseko Ntondini.

My appreciation goes to all the paddlers with whom I have shared training, competition and sunsets at Emmarentia Dam – from Wits, Dabulamanzi and the Soweto Canoe and Recreation Club. Thanks to my partners on the Dusi River over the years – Jim Davies, Grant Wilson, Shaun Rubenstein, Russell Willis, Jacques Theron, Mike Stewart, Siseko Ntondini, Shelley Cruickshanks, Craig Turton and Thulani Mbanjwa – for enduring my company on the water.

And thanks to the many seconds and helpers in my paddling career, particularly my brothers – Dominic, Alexander and Grahame – as well as Bulky Stothard and Terry Clark.

Acknowledgements

Sincere thanks to my colleagues at Kingsmead College for much support in my paddling and writing, particularly to my boss, Lisa Kaplan, and to Saartjie Venter for giving me time to be involved in the *Beyond the River* film.

Thank you to all those who have contributed in some way to this book.

For sharing the dream and insisting that the film and book were possible, indeed inevitable, I thank Brad Fisher, without whom there would not have been a Soweto Canoe Club, film or book.

And for sharing your, my, our journey, I thank Siseko Ntondini.